NLP FOR TRAINERS

Latest titles in the McGraw-Hill Training Series

Details of these and other titles in the series are available from:

The Product Manager, Professional Books, McGraw-Hill Book Company Europe,
Shoppenhangers Road, Maidenhead, Berkshire SL6 2QL, United Kingdom
Tel: 01628 23432 Fax: 01628 770224

NLP for Trainers

Communicating for excellence

Harry Alder

McGRAW-HILL BOOK COMPANY

London · New York · St Louis · San Francisco · Auckland
Bogotá · Caracas · Lisbon · Madrid · Mexico · Milan
Montreal · New Delhi · Panama · Paris · San Juan · São Paulo
Singapore · Sydney · Tokyo · Toronto

Published by
McGRAW-HILL Book Company Europe
Shoppenhangers Road, Maidenhead, Berkshire, SL6 2QL, England
Telephone: 01628 23432
Fax: 01628 770224

British Library Cataloguing in Publication Data
Alder, Harry
  NLP for trainers:
  communicating for excellence. – (McGraw-Hill training
  series)
  1. Neurolinguistic programming 2. Employees – Training of
  I. Title
  658.3'1244

  ISBN 0 07 709134 5

Library of Congress Cataloging-in-Publication Data

Alder, Harry
    NLP for trainers: communicating
  for excellence/Harry Alder
      p. cm. — (McGraw-Hill training series)
    ISBN 0-07-709134-5 (pbk. : alk. paper)
    1. Employees—Training of. 2. Communication in management.
  3. Neurolinguistic programming. I. Title. II. Series.
  HF5549.5.T7A45
  658.3'124—dc20   95-4979C
                                                         CIP

McGraw-Hill
A Division of The McGraw·Hill Companies

12345 CUP9876

Typeset by BookEns Limited, Royston, Herts.
and printed and bound in Great Britain at the University Press, Cambridge.
Printed on permanent paper in compliance with ISO Standard 9706.

To Thomas and Charlotte

Contents

Series preface

Training and development are now firmly centre stage in most organizations, if not all. Nothing unusual in that—for some organizations. They have always seen training and development as part of the heart of their businesses—but more and more must see it that same way.

The demographic trends through the 1990s will inject into the marketplace severe competition for good people who will need good training. Young people without conventional qualifications, skilled workers in redundant crafts, people out of work, women wishing to return to work—all will require excellent training to fit them to meet the job demands of the 1990s and beyond.

But excellent training does not spring from what we have done well in the past. T&D specialists are in a new ball game. 'Maintenance' training—training to keep up skill levels to do what we have always done—will be less in demand. Rather, organization, work and market change training are now much more important and will remain so for some time. Changing organizations and people is no easy task, requiring special skills and expertise which, sadly, many T&D specialists do not possess.

To work as a 'change' specialist requires us to get to centre stage—to the heart of the company's business. This means we have to ask about future goals and strategies, and even be involved in their development, at least as far as T&D policies are concerned.

This demands excellent communication skills, political expertise, negotiating ability, diagnostic skills—indeed, all the skills a good internal consultant requires.

The implications for T&D specialists are considerable. It is not enough merely to be skilled in the basics of training, we must also begin to act like business people and to think in business terms and talk the language of business. We must be able to resource training not just from within but by using the vast array of external resources. We must be able to manage our activities as well as any other manager. We must share in the creation and communication of the company's vision. We must never let the goals of the company out of our sight.

In short, we may have to grow and change with the business. It will be hard. We shall have to demonstrate not only relevance but also value for money and achievement of results. We shall be our own boss, as accountable for results as any other line manager, and we shall have to deal with fewer internal resources.

The challenge is on, as many T&D specialists have demonstrated to me over the past few years. We need to be capable of meeting that challenge. This is why McGraw-Hill Book Company Europe have planned and launched this major new training series—to help us meet that challenge.

The series covers all aspects of T&D and provides the knowledge base from which we can develop plans to meet the challenge. They are practical books for the professional person. They are a starting point for planning our journey into the twenty-first century.

Use them well. Don't just read them. Highlight key ideas, thoughts, action pointers or whatever, and have a go at doing something with them. Through experimentation we evolve; through stagnation we die.

I know that all the authors in the McGraw-Hill Training Series would want me to wish you good luck. Have a great journey into the twenty-first century.

ROGER BENNETT
Series Editor

About the series editor

Roger Bennett has over 20 years' experience in training, management education, research and consulting. He has long been involved with trainer training and trainer effectiveness. He has carried out research into trainer effectiveness, and conducted workshops, seminars, and conferences on the subject around the world. He has written extensively on the subject including the book *Improving Trainer Effectiveness*, Gower. His work has taken him all over the world and has involved directors of companies as well as managers and trainers.

Dr Bennett has worked in engineering, several business schools (including the International Management Centre, where he launched the UK's first masters degree in T&D), and has been a board director of two companies. He is the editor of the *Journal of European Industrial Training* and was series editor of the ITD's *Get In There* workbook and video package for the managers of training departments. He now runs his own business called The Management Development Consultancy.

Acknowledgements

I would like to thank Miles Peacock, an NLP Master Practitioner, for several helpful comments that were incorporated into the early manuscript. Ian Newton and Liz Burns, NLP Master Trainers with *Stenhouse Consultancy*, and Beryl Heather, Master Trainer with *Realisation*, also gave personal help and support for which I am grateful.

1 Introduction

Neuro-Linguistic Programming (NLP) has gained ground remarkably in recent years, its influence being felt in more and more areas. It is, however, still relatively new, and many training practitioners have little or no knowledge of its existence. This book, which assumes that readers have no prior knowledge of the subject, is both an introduction and a basic practical manual on NLP from the point of view of training and development. Based on my own understanding of NLP and its use both in a wide context and in my own training and development practice, I have tried to identify what NLP has to offer the world of training. At the same time I have suggested how NLP can in turn draw on the problems and issues of training and development (which I shall refer to as T&D) and adapt its techniques further, to help trainers in a practical way.

NLP has proved to be particularly successful in the areas of personal development and communication. It has all but transformed communication theory, and its emphasis on 'what actually works' is a welcome change in a field rich with theory and rhetoric. It is not my aim to make a case for NLP *per se*—that has been done elsewhere. As a training and development practitioner, rather than an NLP practitioner, I am a *user* of NLP, and have written this book on behalf of potential T&D users. My book *NLP: The New Art and Science of Getting What You Want* (Piatkus, 1994) is a layperson's introduction; but a book by Joseph O'Connor and John Seymour, *Introducing Neuro-Linguistic Programming* (Harper Collins, 1990), has become a standard British text on the subject. My aim here is to present the subject of NLP to those who are involved in any aspect of T&D—as programme designers, directors, consultants, trainers or managers whose responsibility includes part or all of the function.

I have resisted the temptation to offer definitions and discuss the boundaries of 'training' and 'development'—I leave that task to the professional bodies; but, however defined, it is universally seen as critical to business and organizational success. The function takes many forms and is spread widely in terms of where it fits in an organization, what label it is given, and whether provision is internal or external. It is therefore not easy to identify all who might benefit. A line manager might have minimal formal T&D responsibility, but nevertheless gain a lot from what NLP has to say about communicating with staff and customers, and from the less obvious aspects of developing people to higher levels of ability, as distinct from training for specific job skills. But the nature of the subject makes it as useful for the human resources (HR) director or manager or full-time T&D manager as for the stand-up trainer, or functional or line manager. NLP opens up a new world of awareness, and to date there seems to be no area of human endeavour that cannot benefit from its principles and applications. T&D, with its emphasis on people, learning and communication, is set to benefit from NLP more than most.

The aims of this book are:

- to introduce the subject of NLP—in particular to training and human resource development professionals, whether operating inside companies and other organizations or as consultants or other 'outside' providers;
- to explore its implications for and practical application to T&D specifically, and personal development in its widest sense;
- to offer T&D practitioners some powerful personal development tools that they can use themselves, both inside and outside their professional life;
- to place NLP in an overall T&D context, as part of a portfolio of tools available to trainers through this unique series of training guides.

The art and science of personal excellence

Neuro-Linguistic Programming is concerned with how top people in different fields obtain outstanding results, and how their successful thinking and behaviour patterns can be copied. It is concerned with what happens when we *think*, and the effect of our thinking on our own behaviour, and on that of others. It shows us how we can improve our thinking, and thus achieve more. NLP teaches us how to communicate, inwardly and outwardly, in a way that can make the difference between mediocrity and excellence. But, rather than simply adding more to the theory of communication, NLP is also very practical. It models the way outstanding performers think and act, in a form that you and I can use to bring about similar outstanding results. Most of the techniques described in this book can be tried immediately, so you can enjoy getting results while learning, then build on your successes.

NLP is very adaptable. If a particular technique does not give instant results, it allows you to change what you do and the way you think about your specific circumstance or problem until you achieve what you are after. Once you have grasped a few fundamental principles, you can make these changes easily, thereby gaining a better understanding of the way you as an individual think, and the way your thought processes affect your behaviour—and consequently your achievements. NLP provides a whole range of mental techniques for change that enable you to take control of your personal and professional life.

NLP is both an art and a science of personal excellence. It is an art, because the way we think and act is unique to each of us, and any description—especially of feelings, attitudes and beliefs—is bound to be highly subjective. It is also a science, although still embryonic, because it incorporates well-researched methods that can be used to identify the patterns of successful behaviour.

It all started in the early 1970s when John Grinder, a linguist, and Richard Bandler, a mathematician, psychotherapist and computer expert, studied the methods of three leading psychotherapists—Milton H. Erickson, Virginia Satir and Fritz Peris—who were consistently able to bring about outstanding changes in human behaviour. Erickson has been described as one of the greatest hypnotherapists of all time, while Virginia Satir is an outstanding family therapist who has been able to bring about resolutions of seemingly insurmountable relationship problems. Fritz Peris, an innovative psychotherapist, is the founder of Gestalt therapy. Gregory Bateson, a British anthropologist, as well as providing a model of outstanding performance, also greatly influenced the early work of Grinder and Bandler. The methods they developed have since been applied in the fields of sport, business, government and personal development, attracting a large and growing worldwide following.

The impact of NLP has already been far-reaching, as applications have been found in more and more areas of human life. Its simple but profound concepts and track record of practical success have resulted in its remarkable growth, and it now challenges the position of orthodox psychology in its relevance to ordinary people. At the same time it renders generations of self-development and positive thinking books very incomplete and dated.

Although the subject is relatively new, there is no shortage of literature. However, many of the books only cover specific aspects of NLP and can be intimidating to the novice. Many of these were written by authors with backgrounds in psychotherapy or hypnotherapy and the style of the literature reflects this. Not surprisingly, jargon has evolved, partly reflecting the specialized backgrounds of the concept's originators (a linguist and a psychologist) and partly to express some of the new and specialized ideas that any science accumulates. Even in everyday conversation a so-called NLP practitioner might refer to an effective technique as 'elegant' or to the rapport between individuals as a 'dance'. Little has been written for business people, the person in the street, or professional groups such as trainers, the choice being largely limited to either shallow, popularized versions of the subject, or full-blown textbooks on different aspects. This book will, I hope, fill the gap as far as trainers and HR specialists are concerned. It includes the main principles and a number of proven techniques you can use immediately.

It would not have been possible to cover the whole subject in a volume of this size, so I have had to be selective. In this selection process I have taken an attitude of healthy scepticism and have excluded anything that seemed 'hard to swallow' or 'a bit heavy'. Some NLP methods are more appropriate for a therapy situation, and are excluded because they do not fit my DIY requirement. But if you are new or fairly new to NLP, I hope you will find here as much as you can usefully use in a few months, and certainly enough to bring about fundamental improvements in goal-achievement, personal confidence and lifestyle. For those who want to know more, further reading has been suggested at the end of the book.

Why the name?   The *Neuro* part of NLP refers to the neurological processes of seeing, hearing, feeling, tasting and smelling—the senses that we use for inner thought processes as well as for experiencing the outside world. All our understanding, and what we describe as consciousness, comes through these neural windows to our brain. *Linguistic* recognizes the part that language plays, both in our communication with others and in how we organize our thoughts. NLP helps us to use everyday language for better thinking and more successful behaviour. *Programming* refers to the way we can programme our own thoughts and behaviour, much as a computer is programmed to do specific things.

In summary, NLP deals with the way we filter, through our five senses, our experiences of the outside world, and how we use those same inner senses, both intentionally and unintentionally, to achieve the results that we desire. It all revolves around how we perceive or think, and it is our thinking—perception, imagination, values, patterns of belief—that determines what we do and what we achieve. The subject is evolving rapidly as new discoveries are continually being made about the workings of the brain, so any explanation is almost certain to be incomplete. However, for the time being NLP can be defined as 'the art and science of personal excellence'.

NLP and training and development

Let us now consider some of the areas in which NLP can make a significant contribution to training and development. These areas will be referred to at different points in the book as NLP topics and techniques are explained.

Communication   NLP is essentially a structured approach to communication in its widest sense, involving mental as well as behavioural strategies; and communication is what T&D is all about—communicating knowledge, understanding, skills and, hopefully, attitudes to further both an individual's development and some corporate or other goal. Quite simply, any professional communicator needs to be aware of what is on offer—the principles and techniques that are used by experts in communication (sometimes unknowingly), as elicited by NLP techniques. Trainers need to be aware of NLP's contribution to communication theory and practice, and how and when it can be applied in programme design and in the seminar room. An effective trainer is an effective communicator. It can be argued that communication skills outweigh technical subject knowledge in importance (and this applies just as much to selling or public speaking as to training) when trying to get across a 'message'. Thus it can be seen that the potential returns in communication effectiveness through the use of NLP techniques are high.

Practicality   NLP is supremely practical. Its premises are based on what works, rather than what sounds convincing. Its few principles, or presuppositions, are not so much 'true' as 'useful'. Moreover, NLP engages in a continuous search for a better way. It is adaptive, dynamic and pragmatic, and should appeal to most feet-on-the-ground professionals. In the pages that follow you will find lots of things to test, skills to learn, and techniques to apply and adapt. And if something does not work, NLP offers ways of generating plenty of other approaches in the continuing search for effectiveness. This makes any learning readily transferable to the work situation—games and simulations are not involved, so there is no gap to be bridged in terms of the relevance to real life at work and in the home. The problem of transferring skills back into the workplace is one of the biggest weaknesses of conventional training programmes.

Cost-effectiveness   The highly pragmatic and results-based nature of NLP is appealing to the training provider who has to justify his or her function—as is becoming increasingly the case. Sometimes results—and quick results—have to be identified to justify a time and financial investment. Contrary to the purist, longer term view of personal development, financial appraisal is part of contemporary business, and NLP makes a stronger than average case when its results are evaluated. It has much to say about 'outcomes', so lives happily with an approach to T&D that is aligned to objectives, and the cost of achieving them. This provides a timely emphasis on training 'outputs' rather than 'inputs'.

In 1991 the Royal Society of Arts mounted a series of consultations under the label 'Learning Pays', suggesting a number of impediments to learning in UK society, and offering solutions. The emphasis was on 'learning how to learn' rather than dependence upon teachers, and the strongest recurring themes of the research concerned attitudes and aspirations. NLP has made a major contribution in this area, similarly emphasizing self-development. As well as recognizing the importance of attitudes, NLP is also able to bring about the cognitive changes upon which learning depends.

A sound theoretical base

This is not to underestimate the importance of NLP in adding to the theoretical base of communication, personal development and learning. While it is involved closely with the fickle and sometimes anarchical laboratory of the human mind, NLP—having structures and jargon as does any technical field of study and practice—comes as close as any cognitive subject to a science. Its pedigree is sound, and its significance in the field of psychotherapy, as well as sport, business and learning, gives it a credibility that mainstream psychology and earlier 'positive thinking' often did not attain. It therefore appeals to hard thinkers and innate sceptics who need to place their T&D in a strategic, philosophical or theoretical frame.

Personal excellence and empowerment

NLP has also earned the label of 'the science of personal excellence'. It majors on the individual, not as a corporate or institutional chattel, but as a total, unique person. This is the latent human potential that the current vogue of empowerment rightly seeks to harness. As the professional guardians of this vital empowerment ideal, the HR manager, the management developer and the trainer can each borrow much from NLP.

The 1980s' search for 'corporate excellence' was doomed to fail—excellence always lay in individual people, not in inanimate corporations. Anecdotal evidence easily supports the role of outstanding individuals at the top of organizations in creating their successful cultures and results (this is covered in my book *Think Like a Leader* (Piatkus), which drew on 200 interviews with top business leaders). But the massive gains surely lie in empowering the whole workforce. My research for that book showed wide agreement that the extent to which this personal creativity and motivation can be stimulated and channelled to the mutual benefit of both the individual and company will dictate corporate success in the coming decades.

While deserving the full attention of top management, much of the outworking of such a vision will fall to the training and development function—to which this book is directed. It would seem, therefore, that personal excellence is high on the corporate agenda, and NLP has a lot to offer.

Other contemporary changes in the world of human resources make NLP attractive. More enlightened organizations are moving away from the idea of people as a human resource, along with other business resources such as plant and money, to see people in a far more special, indeed unique, way. Such a view is of people who are uniquely creative, with lives that extend beyond office hours and the company building, and beyond the immediate economic interests of an institution. This is the holistic view of the individual, in which true personal effectiveness is not compartmentalized but pervades every area of life. So the search for true empowerment (as distinct from corporate rhetoric) is the very essence of NLP. By addressing feelings, attitudes and beliefs, rather than just overt nine-to-five behaviour, it has much to say about motivation and personal achievement, whether inside or outside the corporation. The T&D function should be well placed, using NLP technology, to help businesses and public sector organizations achieve the empowerment they see as fundamental to success.

Learning   NLP has made a contribution to learning theory and practice. Impressive results, such as in the learning of spelling in the case of dyslexic people, are based on the understanding we have of 'thinking strategies', which have been found to apply wherever we find 'excellence' in human achievement. In 'helping people to learn', rather than 'teaching' or even 'training', trainers can try out some of the successful strategies in different areas of skills training, and develop new ones using NLP models.

Outcomes   NLP concerns outcomes—goals, objectives, the fulfilment of desires. As a subject, this is far from unique, as any goal-oriented professional from almost any area will assert, but it offers remarkable ways to increase the likelihood of achieving a given outcome. Its emphasis on results links inputs with outputs in a cybernetic sense, drawing on known characteristics of the human brain and central nervous system, rather than (just) 'positive affirmations' or other earlier forms of goal definition and reinforcement. It adds internal representation, or what might be termed visualization, as a further powerful tool in triggering this cybernetic success mechanism.

Goal orientation, while present in the content of many successful training programmes, is not always crucial in the training experience *per se*—that is, it is not always clear what the training is intended to achieve. In the absence of outcome yardsticks and criteria for evaluating effectiveness, the training function has sometimes been guilty of equating bigger training budgets or hours of training (inputs) with training success. This might be excused on the grounds of 'any training is better than no training', 'training is good', or simply the short-term survival of the function. But effectiveness has got to be evaluated in terms of outputs—'outcomes' to use the more all-embracing jargon—however embryonic our understanding of 'effectiveness' in the more holistic context of true empowerment.

There is therefore room for more outcome-based training and development strategies. Objectives need to be set and monitored in a context which is specific to the person, team or learning strategy, or to financial, strategic, corporate or other criteria. NLP has a contribution to make in clarifying the key issues in this complex set of relationships. Personal outcomes, for instance, will have to be reconciled with higher functional or corporate outcomes. NLP specifically addresses the reconciliation of such conflicting outcomes.

Models of excellence

NLP developed the concept of modelling excellent performance. As we have seen, its origins were concentrated on modelling the behaviour of known outstanding excellent practitioners in the field of psychotherapy, although its field of study widened rapidly. So-called 'strategies' can be emulated, so that a 'mediocre' person can become a master in a skill or behaviour. This is an entire field of training that can influence the way skills are acquired. The T&D programme designer might wish to incorporate modelling as part of a portfolio of training mechanisms. The trainer, at the same time, might wish to model 'excellent' communicators (such as outstanding sales trainers) personally. Like public speakers in other fields, trainers need something special, to be memorable and to stand out from the masses; and these qualities on the part of the trainer, when honed to the level of 'unconscious competence', might far override content in contributing to the effectiveness of a training event.

The trainer, like any other professional, needs to continuously enhance his or her skills as a practitioner. If learning is to be continuous, then all in the business need to keep learning. There is a danger of stagnation when a stand-up training presentation no longer inspires enthusiasm. The principles of NLP provide useful and sometimes disarming 'tests' of personal excellence. NLP offers enough DIY techniques to allow you to fill any gaps, and rise to new levels of competence.

This is not a training manual, but rather an introduction to NLP written particularly for trainers. I have therefore assumed that the reader has a reasonable level of knowledge and experience of training and development, but no knowledge of NLP. As I have consequently had to be selective about what could be included in a single volume on the subject of NLP, allotting space to general training topics—although tempting, as I have my views—was out of the question. If your knowledge is lacking in areas such as learning styles, presentation skills, or recent political developments in training, for example, there are other books on those subjects. I have also avoided being too prescriptive in applying NLP principles and techniques to T&D. Although some of the examples are drawn from the familiar world of training, you would do better to make any associations and spot applications yourself—which is more in the spirit of NLP in any case. The same key principles might be applied very differently from one training practitioner to another, all with beneficial results. Even specific techniques have been used for very different purposes, again giving benefit while also extending the reach of the subject. So I have left you, as an enlightened, professional reader, to apply the principles and use the techniques as you wish. Too much prescription would reduce the very richness and adaptability of the subject, which is in any event dynamic and constantly growing; you should therefore constantly ask yourself such questions as: What does this mean for me? How can this help? In what situations can I try that technique? How can I adapt this exercise to meet my specific needs? In this way you will gain more from the book than by following a manual of NLP-based training devices. In short, you will have to do some thinking, and that is what NLP is all about.

2 Principles and presuppositions

NLP offers a number of presuppositions. These are not as rigid as scientific laws or theories, partly because of the subjective nature of what is being studied (i.e. how we as people think) and partly because that is the way NLP treats them—not so much as inviolable, or even true, but *useful*. These presuppositions are quite few and simple. Their power lies in how they can change our attitudes and feelings about something, and, in there application to widely different situations, bring about actual change. To bring about major changes, there is first a need to be *aware* of the potential for change in any interpersonal situation. It starts, as with anything, with what we believe, or expect—how we think. Then we need to have an understanding of the process that applies in achieving any outcome, including a communication. NLP has identified such a process—or sequence of stages—that seems to apply universally and consistently produces results, and it is into this framework of simple steps that the presuppositions are applied.

A formula for success

This four-stage process, or cycle, which might well be termed a formula for success, will be outlined first. Consider how you can apply each stage both personally and professionally. Try to translate each into a training context.

1. Know what you want

The first stage is to know what you want. This requirement is by no means unique to NLP and has long been accepted as an important factor in personal and business success. In addressing trainers I have taken for granted the importance of a goal-oriented approach to achievement and problem solving, although I refer to earlier research evidence in a previous book. NLP does, however, suggest ways to get these desires, goals or objectives—whatever you want to call them—into a clear and achievable form. Many people have a lot of unfulfilled desires that turn out not to be 'well formed', and this accounts for much of their apparent failure, whatever the techniques used to bring about achievement of the goals. A clear goal gives you a head start to success in any field. An understanding of how the mind seems to 'handle' these goals also helps. We know, for example, that a desire that is strongly visualized or pictured in the mind—or more specifically *sensed* inwardly, with the sounds and feelings as well as the visual image—is more likely to come about than a goal that is, say, just spoken or written down but not clearly 'experienced' within. This is well known in a sports setting where the intended goal is seldom in doubt and (such as a medal ceremony) is easily visualized. It is far less common in business and management, although it is certainly borne out in the case of achievers in just about any field.

Although this process involving clear goals is part of how we think as individuals, even a cursory consideration of business and other organizations will show that goal-orientation—knowing what you want—is also a universal factor in corporate success. Training and development, along with every other aspect of an organization, is subject to this process in which you have first to decide where you want to go or what you want to achieve. Using a combination of common sense and knowledge of how the brain handles the thoughts involved, your 'hit rate' of success can be increased dramatically simply by getting this first stage right. The term 'outcome' is used to include goals, desires and intentions, so the first step is to have a clearly defined outcome. In the next chapter I shall suggest several 'tests' for a good outcome, and explore further the whole matter of personal and work goals.

2. Act   The next part of the process is to act. Do something that you think will bring about your desired outcome. Again this is common sense, but we soon discover that most unfulfilled goals, both individually and corporately, have not been seriously attempted. They remain as wishes, pipedreams, theories or even detailed plans. In many cases they depend on other people or circumstances, so our alibi for non-achievement stays intact—we have plenty of excuses. The process of achieving what you want is part of a continuous process involving feedback. It is a system that can only be successful if all the parts are working, and each part is as important as any other. In this case getting on and doing something is as important as knowing what you want to achieve. For example, a missile must initially be fired in the general direction of the target. It may appear to weave around meaninglessly at first, but it increasingly adopts a course that will reach the predefined target. It has to go *somewhere* before it can sense how far it is off track, and make whatever correction is necessary. So even if what you do first does not work, it is essential to make a start.

3. Notice what happens   The next stage involves noticing what happens when you do what you are doing. This is a familiar concept to engineers involved in cybernetic systems like robots where, only by knowing the results of a particular programmed activity can you know what you have to do differently to get closer to what you want to achieve. As individuals we call upon all our senses—mainly seeing , hearing and feeling—to be aware of the results of any action. NLP uses the term 'sensory acuity', and this involves as much skill as any activity in the previous 'doing' stage. Because it is less obviously a skill, however, and not as easily observed by others as an outward behaviour, it is rarely done well. To some it seems passive, and involves too much thinking. A large part of NLP is creating this sensitivity to what is happening around us, sometimes using senses that have not been used much in this way or to the high degree needed. Then the logic is simple: the more you can spot what effect your actions have in bringing you closer to what you want, the greater the chance of taking corrective action—doing something different—and so finally achieving what you want. Our sensory systems are unbelievably sophisticated so we each have all the resources needed for this feedback stage. We may, however, need some direction and practice before it becomes an instinctive part of our goal-achieving. Sometimes we have to open our minds to get a better perception of what is happening and this may require us to 'reframe' a situation. The idea of reframing, and specific techniques you can use to get an added perspective on a situation, is covered in Chapter 6.

4. Be flexible

This naturally brings us to the final part of the process. You must be prepared to *change* what you are doing, and if necessary keep changing until you achieve the desired result. So there is an inherent flexibility in the NLP approach to goal achievement and problem solving—a humility of sorts—that is not too common in everyday institutionalized behaviour, including businesses. In fact the concept is alien to many organizations. When something does not work, the tendency is to do more of the same thing—maybe more quickly, more cheaply, more accurately—but essentially the same thing. In other words, trying to do the same thing better. NLP says try something *different*. Do not try harder at what you are doing if it is patently not producing the results you want, even if you have invested a lot of money and pride in your present course of action.

This flexibility is part of the total process, and no single stage makes much practical sense without the others. Much conventional training is carried out with little thought of changing what is done other than cosmetically, or in terms of greater efficiency, which usually means doing the same thing more efficiently (according to some economic or accounting criterion such as cost per person per day's training). But unless clear objectives have been set as to the purpose of the training— why, for instance, money is being spent on this course rather than on some capital project, higher salaries or better working conditions— change is unlikely to happen. The training is ineffective. Worse than this, human nature will allow training 'inputs' to grow and take on a life of their own as long as money can be obtained from the business, regardless of the training's relevance to the goals of the organization or the function the training seeks to serve. And the longer and more entrenched the process, the less likely is the ongoing change that is vital for success or even survival in a changing environment. So feedback sensitivity only makes sense in the light of knowing what you want to achieve in the first place and a willingness to change if you are not achieving it.

The process can be summarized as follows:

Clear goals + Sensory acuity + Action + Flexibility = OUTCOMES

Some presuppositions

Within this simple process the principles or *presuppositions* of NLP operate. As with the four-stage success formula, I shall explain how these apply in everyday situations both personally and in your training role.

The map is not the territory

This presupposition uses the familiar analogy of a map to illustrate a very profound principle. What we each perceive as reality—the world to which we relate—is in fact our very personal interpretation of the world. Our understanding is *filtered*, not just by our five senses which might produce a different interpretation to another person, but by our existing store of memories, values, beliefs, background and all the things that make us unique and different to the next person. So we each have a personal perceptual map of 'reality'. The fact that these maps are different becomes very obvious when tackling so-called communication problems, in which 'facts' are construed very differently and thus produce different feelings, emotions and behaviour. A heavy rainstorm might be good or bad, and might make you happy or unhappy, depending on how you perceive it—through your personal perceptual map of the real rainstorm. Your 'interpretation' is no better or worse than anyone else's, it has simply been subject to different filters.

None of us can actually know what reality is as there are limitations to our sensing abilities. For example, we can just detect a tiny part of the various energy waves that come to us in the form of light or sound, but we also edit, largely unconsciously, whatever comes through the windows of our senses according to earlier, similarly filtered patterns of thought. What we experience, therefore, is more like a map, however detailed and rich its content, than the real world outside—the territory. The eyewitness accounts of a traffic accident well illustrate the richness and variety of individual maps. We just see things differently. And the greater the emotional content in any behaviour or communication, the greater the likelihood of differences in perception.

Communication then becomes an attempt to understand the other person's map—'how they tick', as we would say—and to express our own map so that they understand how we have interpreted the same outside world. Such a presupposition involves some humility and mutual respect, as none of us is able to claim that we know reality, but only that we have a unique subjective interpretation of it.

The fact that our maps differ accounts for all manner of communication problems, from marriage breakdown to racial bigotry and war. It also produces the rich diversity of human behaviour, and the splendour of art and literature. Any agreement or similarity (neat examples like 'that is a house' or 'the traffic light shows red' are the exception rather than the rule) accounts for the fact that, to a greater or lesser degree, we survive as a society from one day to the next with different maps of the same territory.

Every behaviour has a positive intention

NLP sees all behaviour as *purposeful*; that is, it intends to bring about a certain outcome, which, at least to the individual behaving, is positive. When viewed objectively, much of our behaviour does not make sense, in that it does not seem to be 'right' either for society (in the case of destructive or socially unacceptable behaviour) or even for the individual. For example, a person might continue to smoke in the full knowledge of the likely health consequences. But it does not take much reflection to understand that things are rarely that simple, and there may well be other factors such as peer recognition, relief from anxiety, or pleasure which are not just other outcomes but are construed by the person as being positive rather than negative. Apparently irrational behaviour may reflect an individual's conflicting outcomes, and the difficulty of balancing perceived pleasure and perceived pain. In some cases the positive intention may not be easy to identify, especially by that individual. But NLP maintains, nevertheless, that such a positive intention exists.

A so-called terrorist (described according to another person's mental map as a freedom fighter, patriot, murderer, or whatever) will inevitably give some positive reason for his or her behaviour. There is always *purpose*, however misguided that purpose may be. As far as the individual's goal-achieving behaviour is concerned, the behaviour—like any behaviour—is 'guided' cybernetically towards a positive, purposeful outcome. In some context or other—and certainly according to the individual's map—it makes sense.

Students or trainees might behave in ways that do not seem conducive to learning, or fit the objectives of an expensive, carefully designed programme. Their behaviour might seem to be illogical from any, including their own, point of view. But some other intention will always be present. Based upon this presupposition, it would be naïve on the part of a trainer or employer to assume common objectives on the part of a whole group of individuals, when even one individual is likely to have several, probably unconscious 'intentions'.

Once we can identify a positive intention, even a minor change in what we do can make our communication more effective. This is an important principle in the achievement of goals and objectives. For instance, if it can be shown that there is another way to achieve an intention, without disproportionate pain or negative consequences, then behaviour can be readily changed, however habitual it may be. If, for example, the relief from anxiety, or the macho image that smoking gives, could be obtained in another way that did not have health hazards, then such a way would on balance be more effective. Understanding a behaviour may require us to identify the positive intention. There may well be another way of achieving it—or several ways, one of which can be chosen. If the 'freedom fighter' can be convinced that there is another way to achieve his or her purposes— perhaps by political or economic means—a change in behaviour might well result. But as long as an outcome is present—conscious or unconscious—behaviour of any sort will follow. It will usually 'make sense' to the behaver. And in pursuing a positive intention, of course, it does make sense. Denying the reality of an outcome of unacceptable or inexplicable behaviour may perhaps give us the pleasure of maintaining the moral high ground, but is unlikely to change the offending behaviour. Such denial fails to understand the purposeful nature of human behaviour, and so is ineffective in changing it.

The presupposition can be applied to any area of behaviour, including training and, even more widely, learning. Where the behaviour of a trainee, for example, suggests belligerence, laziness, anarchy or whatever, it is tempting for the trainer to rationalize the situation (to make excuses) in some way and so feel no responsibility to change the method of training. Thus there is neither the determination to achieve the outcome—the goal of a successful training intervention—nor the recognition that a different approach might bring a different outcome.

The principle adds further to the need for sensory acuity in noticing where goals are not being achieved. It will no doubt require acuity to see beyond outward meaningless or belligerent behaviour to a positive intention. Such intention might be to impress peers, be popular, display independence and freedom of expression, have a good time, avoid promotion, or whatever. Each of these intentions, positive and reasonable to the trainee (if he or she is conscious of them) can probably be achieved in other ways, and in some cases the trainer can help. But the likelihood of some positive intention must first be at least entertained, or the trainer's mind will remain closed to what is really happening and what might be done to turn the situation round to achieve the respective goals of trainer and trainee alike.

The principle can just as easily apply to an organization. Let us assume that the MD or finance director has summarily slashed the training budget. This seems irrational to the training director who is convinced of the value of the training, and his or her personal indispensability. The MD, however, might be subject to a parent company injunction for short-term results, or be applying a wider development strategy that avoids the duplication of some resources. Sadly, individual functions tend to plough their own furrow and see their peers with the same perceptual blinkers with which someone witnesses a traffic accident. With reasonable management training, however, any professional in human resources, marketing or production should be able to see things from a business or corporate viewpoint, from which perspective an apparent anti-functional behaviour can usually be seen in a better light. Understanding the positive intention, which in this case might be a short-term improvement in overall expenditure by reducing indirect costs, might lead to other ways of achieving it. Some training, for example, might well meet the short-term, bottom-line criteria. Specific training to bring about sales improvements, inventory reduction, debtors and other working capital reduction, or cost savings such as in energy or stationary, are possible examples. Meaningful training, based on outputs rather than inputs, and that recognizes the reality of the organization's objectives, might also produce better, more resourceful managers. Once we start asking the right questions about intentions, it is just a matter of time before we obtain the right answers. So the T&D function must be aware of higher level corporate and business outcomes, as well as unarticulated outcomes on the part of trainees.

The biggest changes brought about by NLP tend to be in the person most in control of the situation. So what can the trainer gain from understanding and applying this presupposition? This is the most difficult area in which to apply the principle. In what way is one's own behaviour influenced by underlying intentions that may not be fully recognized? Most of us have aspects of our behaviour that we would like to change, and these are likely to cover work and professional situations as well as behaviour at a personal and social level. Some behaviours seem impossible to change and form, it seems, part of our personality. Understanding the intention that these behaviours are attempting to bring about will create choices—other ways of achieving the same intentions which are more acceptable to us, and indeed to those who are affected by our behaviour.

A primary school teacher who is fresh from training, and going through the traumatic fast learning curve of the early weeks as a school teacher talked of the difficulty of keeping the children quiet. Left to their own devices, the children seemed capable of more or less unlimited decibels. She quickly learned not to react by competing in volume, but in an attempt to understand the situation she used sensory acuity to watch and listen. She realized, however, that her own intentions to assert her authority, to show that she was in control, or in the longer term to produce good citizens or whatever, could be achieved in other ways. She found, for instance, that by directing her attention and praise to a smaller group of children who were having a good time without the accompanying noise, the classroom cacophony abated almost miraculously. She had formed a perspective on what her outcomes were, and considered whether there was some other way to achieve them—what *choices* she had. The power of an NLP approach is that if her first change of behaviour had not worked, she would have continued to modify her behaviour—trying anything but the yelling and screaming she now knew did not work—until success came. Insight as to the positive intentions on the part of the children would similarly mean a better understanding of the situation, and some change of behaviour on the part of the teacher.

No failure—only feedback

NLP is about learning, and learning is about making mistakes— which is how we usually describe our repeated attempts before we succeed. NLP manages to avoid the emotional and negative connotation of these 'mistakes'. It says there is no failure, only feedback. If a behaviour does not produce the intended results, the information learned (i.e. that a certain behaviour does not produce a desired outcome) is feedback upon which to base a change of behaviour. It is neither good nor bad, just information upon which to base our next step. So 'mistakes' are eliminated. And this is not just semantics. Without what we might call the 'mistake', we could not go on to successful results. It is part of the cybernetic system of success.

Accepting the four-stage success process as necessary for all achievement, we accept any interim happenings as part of the package. Falling short of an initially determined goal is a vital part of this. This can make a dramatic change to your level of achievement. Many people do not even attempt goals because they fear failure. Even a single failure is too much for some people, let alone the many shortfalls that are usually part of the cybernetic process of goal achievement, and with which 'successful' people are only too familiar. Self-esteem can be hit hard by a succession of perceived failures, and a lower self-esteem almost guarantees a self-fulfilling limitation to what we achieve. Anyone who learns to type will not make progress unless they hit lots of wrong keys and produce, in the early stages, a standard that seems to take them right back to childhood. Similarly, if you do not know what it is to oversteer a car when learning to drive, then you have probably not grasped the instinctive skill of steering. However quick we are to learn, we cannot short-cut the process of doing, noticing where we have gone wrong, then making changes to see what effect they have and so on until we master it. In due course, you do not need to think about what you are doing, and this is also one of the secrets of learning and goal achievement that we shall discuss later. For the moment let us say goodbye to failure and mistakes. The only real failure is when you fail to learn from your experience and repeat the same ineffective behaviour.

Any choice is better than no choice

It might be necessary to try different ways before you achieve something. Implicit in all this is choice, and NLP says that any choice is always better than no choice. In seeking alternative ways to bring about a desired outcome, you create choices. The choice of whether to smoke or not to smoke; whether to react emotionally to a certain person in the same way at all times; whether to maintain a present way of life, belief system or personal priorities. Using the map metaphor, you are free to choose your own map: how you interpret the world; the meaning you give to events and circumstances; what you feel about things.

All this is within a person's control; we have more choices than we often care to admit. In this respect, NLP seeks to open up more choices by helping us to see things from other perspectives. We might put it this way: one option is no option; two options may be a dilemma; three or more options give us the freedom to begin to achieve our goals. We have just seen that we have the option to treat what happens to us as mistakes or failures, or as important learning information upon which we base our future behaviour. You have the choice—and if there is another way (and there usually is) to achieve your goals or fulfil your intentions, you are free to take it.

These principles and the techniques you will learn are all intended to increase your choices, and thus your chances of success. This desire for choice is another universal feature of human nature, and is linked with personal rights, self-esteem and freedom. You should be able to see it at work in training situations and see how the principle can be applied. At a very fundamental level, for instance, people value the choice of how they learn. Some just want to bury themselves in books and do not seem to want or need the attentions of a teacher, while others must have personal, face-to-face teaching. Some people will insist on doing practical things, and others will want to understand the underlying theory before they even attempt to apply it. So if greater understanding or skill is the training objective, the learning disposition of the trainee might well be a bigger factor in the training outcome than the actual content or sophistication of delivery of the programme. The perception of the individual—his or her personal map—is critical. Simply by believing you have had a *choice* in the training—whatever the reality— motivation and learning will be enhanced.

As a professional trainer, one of the worst occupational hazards I have had to face is people being *sent* on courses, even when the training fits their job and development needs perfectly. It hardly ever works, and costs companies a small fortune in wasted expenditure. In a number of cases it is counterproductive and people can turn against training (and trainers) for no other reason than they were not offered the basic right to have a choice in their development. I shall refer later to the way training strategies and corporate culture can create a better environment for the actual training programme or event.

The meaning of a communication is the response it produces

Some of these presuppositions overlap and are interrelated. One says that the meaning of your communication is the response it produces. Traditionally communication has been looked upon as a set of models and techniques that help us get our message across through different mediums and at different levels, such as interpersonally or when presenting to a large audience. A lot of the attention has been on the *means*, including the technology that makes communication increasingly sophisticated. But communication is what we do to achieve a certain *outcome*. Unless the outcome is achieved, the communication is ineffective. An earlier presupposition suggested that if a behaviour is seen to be ineffective, you should try something different, and keep trying until you achieve your goal. The importance of this presupposition is that you measure the effectiveness of your communication only by whether it produces the desired response. A company might spend massive amounts of money using outside professionals to make staff aware of the mission and values of the company. If the staff perceive that top management are remote and not to be trusted, and that they as individual workers are not valued, then the communication has failed. As we saw earlier, behaviour is purposeful. We communicate for a purpose; for instance, we might want to inform, warn, impress, influence, persuade, shock, or entertain—or any combination of these. The extent to which we achieve any of these outcomes is the measure of our success. We cannot measure our success by the words we use, or body language, or audio-visual aids, or the number of times we repeat the message.

This changes the whole nature of the art and science of communication. The best communication between people is when there is *rapport*—mutual understanding of perceptual maps—as in the case of close, long-term, personal and work relationships. In these cases communication in its usual sense might be minimal or non-existent. The slightest glance, word, or nuance of body language can convey the clearest meaning. 'Understanding' seems to be communicated without using the outward senses. But it works, and that is what effective communication is all about. To bemoan the fact that 'He would not listen', or 'I made it absolutely clear' as an excuse for not achieving our goals is placing the onus on the communicatee rather than the communicator. NLP, as well as offering choices, puts responsibility on the communicator—the person who wants to achieve the outcome. The young school teacher in the earlier example might easily have blamed the unruly children, but this would not discharge her from her responsibility to produce the outcomes she had decided upon. A training event is a complex exercise in communication. As training professionals we would do well to re-examine the very nature of communication, and subject it to the four-stage goal achievement process we have already seen: (1) decide on what you want; (2) do what you think will bring this about; (3) check whether it works; and if not (4) try something different. Never mind about 'communication' labels. If you do not need to communicate and can still achieve your outcomes you can forget communication. If you can achieve an outcome without training in its conventional sense, then why not?

Conclusions   NLP offers these simple but profound presuppositions. They are neither creeds nor physical laws. They are just useful to know and worth remembering when you want to achieve something. They are foundations upon which the techniques described later in the book are based. An underlying tenet is that of *behaving as if* these presuppositions were true. Thereafter success lies with you, as you apply the presuppositions, understand how you think, and try new approaches in your personal life and in your training capacity. NLP has evolved in this flexible, adaptive way, and will no doubt continue to do so. If something is effective, you will tend to use it more, and discard techniques that do not seem right in your company or environment. But achievement lies in knowing what you want, being skilled in observing the results of your actions, and having the flexibility and sometimes humility to try something else until you are successful. NLP is about a learning state of mind. It is not a management tool, but a way of thinking—a way of life. It is highly pragmatic. Its success lies in the results it gets, not on the grandeur of its theories; and it lies in its simplicity rather than its complexity. As 'the art and science of communication' (one of a number of labels NLP has earned) it is set to make big changes in the world of communication, including training and development.

Successful training

This four-stage 'success model' and the presuppositions can be applied to training situations from the strategic level to day-to-day training room practice. I have already referred to the need for training to form part of a total corporate or organization strategy. In this case the goal requirement applies at the high level, but the same clarity is needed. The T&D function will also have its own hierarchy of objectives, and these should in turn fit the wider human resources function of the company, linked with other 'people' issues such as rewards, recruitment and morale.

A training programme, such as one for developing fast track managers, will similarly be subject to the same need for clear objectives, and the feedback system I have identified. What will be the criteria for success in such a programme? What exactly are we trying to do, and how shall we know we have accomplished it? Or are we at least going in the right direction? But at an even lower level in the hierarchy of goals an individual trainer might reasonably set objectives for an individual course, or a specific exercise or training activity within that course. The same goal-achievement cycle must apply. At this level, however, it might be easier to identify whether an action is producing the desired effect—for example, whether the whole of the group actively participate, whether plenty of ideas are generated or whether the activity produces a particular end result in the form of a written piece or presentation. At an even lower level a simple request on the part of the trainer 'Will you do such-and-such?' is also outcome-based. What is your desired outcome? Will it be clear whether your communication—what you have said and how you said it—has succeeded or not? What will be the evidence? Some action on your part is needed—in this case involving words—but a desired outcome might be achieved by just handing out a document that requires completion, writing something on a flipchart, making some gesture with the hands or even raising the eyebrows. There is then the feedback, and also the willingness to do something different when it is not certain that the outcome has been achieved. All this can happen very quickly and so the 'process' is not easily observable. To complicate matters each side of the communication follows the same pattern—any response on the part of the trainee will also have an outcome (whether or not defined or even conscious, such as to inform or impress or just 'comply') and similar feedback is at work as he or she observes the effect of an answer given. The whole process is dynamic. New outcomes are being formed, and others amended in the light of experience.

3 Achieving outcomes

An outcome might be a goal, objective, desire, purpose or intention. The term appears repeatedly in NLP. The idea of goal-orientation is not unique to NLP, of course, and is central to success in management or any other field, whether viewed personally or organizationally. This was illustrated in research carried out as far back as the 1950s. It was then established that only 3 per cent of a group of high school students had written goals, or thought about their future in such a way. Some 20 years later, the researchers contacted the same group of students, only to learn that the 3 per cent who originally had clear goals accounted for more of the total wealth or asset value than all the rest of the group put together. Although material wealth is hardly a measure of success, it turned out that, even against other more intangible, subjective criteria, the original goal-oriented 3 per cent were the ones who had achieved and fulfilled themselves, not just materially, but in various other ways.

Few businesses can run without some form of goal planning. Other research within business has shown that there is indeed a link between the planning process and eventual outcomes in the form of profits and other business measures. Training and development, as much as any aspect of business, can benefit from a more goal-oriented approach, and NLP has a particular contribution to make in this area.

It will quickly become apparent that the main application of NLP principles and techniques is at a *personal* level—where thinking and perception take priority—and what are termed 'outcomes' embrace personal as well as business or functional goals. But it is obvious to experienced business people in any case that whatever priority corporate, functional or business plans have in an organization, *people* actually own and implement the goals. If a corporate plan is not reflected in the personal outcomes of one or more individuals, it will be sterile indeed—as many are. A legal entity like a company does not share the feelings and attitudes of a fickle and unpredictable individual. But nor does it know of the dreams and vision that can motivate success in the face of any odds, or the awesome creativity that can be tapped. Having said this, the NLP principles and techniques that rightly apply to individuals, can, with a little ingenuity, be readily applied to any organizational goals—including those relating to training and development. As a professional trainer you will benefit both as an individual and also in setting and achieving any programme or functional goals for which you are responsible.

Experienced training professionals who are willing to view the business holistically, rather than from a narrow functional viewpoint, will appreciate the need for clear corporate goals— and the strategy you need to achieve them—and clear functional objectives. This is not to say that it is easy, or indeed possible in every case, to define and subsequently measure the success of a training activity. But the discipline of an 'outcome-oriented' process will at least force this admission, and introduce the sort of balanced judgement that has to be used continuously in risk evaluation in other parts of the business. With such a balanced, corporate perspective, however, a training 'investment' would have to stack up along with any other investment, becoming an integral part of corporate strategy, as it always should have been, but on fair terms.

In times of economic recession—and also, to some extent, in better times—training has to be justified. Not all training is good; not all training is relevant; much training is not viable in a total business context; and most training does not lend itself to quantitative or even qualitative measures. For these reasons, training is often first to be sacrificed in times of difficulty. Training professionals who are concerned with maintaining their budgets at all cost, and whose terms of reference are training inputs rather than outputs, usually operate successfully in better times, especially if they are strong political operators (who, incidentally, NLP can also help). But no one will offer much sympathy when the inevitable demise comes. Greater emphasis on outcomes, especially integration with the corporate mission and strategy, might enhance the designing of 'justifiable', outcome-based training. Even non-training people admit that good training and development is central to business success. NLP can introduce more resilience and credibility into the methods of design and delivery. And a major contribution is the emphasis on outputs.

Inputs and outputs

One of the first distinctions that needs to be made when fixing goals is to understand the difference between an input and an output. Let us assume that you are marketing a forthcoming training event and you need to contact as many potential delegates as possible by letter and then by telephone follow-up. You will probably set yourself a goal— and this is standard time-management wisdom—of, say, making a certain number of calls in an afternoon. You give yourself a goal of 20 calls. Let us assume that you achieve this goal. The question then is what have you really achieved, other than an input towards some output? Your true goal, although it depends upon successful telephone calls, can hardly be measured by the amount of effort or time you give to the activity. Unfortunately effort does not automatically translate into outputs. You might work all week and not get a single course booking.

Imagine that a reasonable hit-rate of telephone calls to bookings on the course is 1:5. A reasonable goal would then be the number of firm bookings you could obtain rather than the time you spend or the number of inputs by way of telephone calls, or, for that matter, letters, or any other kind of *input*. This might not seem an important distinction, but if you had fulfilled all of your planned calls but got no bookings, then in terms of real goals you have achieved nothing— certainly nothing that could contribute to the overall training function and indeed the success of your organization. If, on the other hand, you make *less* telephone calls than your earlier plan, but achieve some actual bookings, then clearly your success rate is higher—that is, you have achieved true outputs and not simply added to your inputs.

The importance of outputs is universal. After the excitement of the game has been forgotten, a soccer match is significant in terms of goals—outputs. And however unfair the ratio of effort to results— inputs to outputs—seems, anyone involved in the game will know where the mind has to be concentrated, and how success will be measured in the final analysis.

Businesses have well-established output criteria in the form of profit expressed as a return on investment or in some other relationship. But below company level, where more subjective cost accounting rather than financial accounting is used, or in an organization that does not measure in profit terms, there is the tendency to confuse inputs and outputs. Training and development operates and is measured at this subcorporate level, and is as divorced as any support function in true 'bottom line'—output—measurement.

Determining inputs and outputs

To determine what is an output and what is an input is not always easy. You need to start at the highest level of goals, which might well be at a corporate, or certainly at a business unit or functional level. The question then is: What am I contributing towards that higher level goal? Clearly, we can spend all our time making telephone calls or writing letters or doing things in a most efficient matter, and yet achieve nothing by way of a contribution to the higher goals of the organization. Therefore, a sensible goal in this case would be some bookings. The target level will vary from individual to individual, which is something we can consider later, but the important thing is that an output has been achieved.

There may be several levels of goal achievement before inputs are converted into the final desired goal of sales, new customers, profit, etc., but the important thing is that value is added, and that you are moving in the right direction towards higher level goals. Also, as direction is more important than pace in achieving worthwhile outcomes, it is important to think in terms of goals at every level, and to ensure that those goals fit into a coherent hierarchy, from the lowest level (in the above case, seeking to achieve success every time a telephone call is made) right up to the organization's mission.

Tests for a good outcome

Having ensured that your goals are true outputs and not inputs, there are several tests that will help you to clarify your goals and increase the probability of success. You will be quite familiar with some of them, which have been part of our management understanding for many years, yet many people still fail to follow basic common sense and thus do not achieve what they are more than capable of achieving. Other tests might be newer to you. As we go through the tests, think about them (1) as applying to you personally, both in work and non-work life; (2) as applying to your training or other work function; (3) in the context of your organization and its planning processes; (4) as a potential part of any training programme; and (5) in the context of individual learning and self-development generally.

Positive

The first rule is to express your goal in positive terms. So, using a personal rather than work example, you would not say, 'I want to lose half a stone,' which is a negative way to express your goal, but rather 'I want to be such and such a weight by Christmas' or by a certain date. This might not seem important, but in fact the way the brain processes thoughts and ideas means that there is more chance of achieving your goal when it is expressed positively than when expressed negatively. List a few goals, some work-based and some personal, and see whether you can express each of them in positive terms. Sometimes you need to use a bit of ingenuity to do this—we form thinking habits as well as physical ones, and it can come as a surprise how often we express things pessimistically or negatively. Yelling at a child 'Don't miss the ball', or 'Don't fall off', has a strange tendency to produce the opposite effect. On balance it is better to know what you are aiming for than what you are avoiding—although both carrots and sticks have a part to play. The simple exercise of positively expressing any outcomes will be worth while and will increase your chances of success. You will be moving *towards* something rather than *away from* something.

One of the best analogies is a cybernetic system, such as a missile or industrial robot—or even a domestic heating system—in which a positive 'target' is always present in the system. And the built-in target—be it 70 degrees room temperature or an enemy tank—is something you *want* rather than the many (in fact, infinite) outcomes you *don't* want.

If I ask you not to think about a dark rain cloud, you will find this impossible. To not do something you have first to understand what it is you have not to do or think about. In practice this involves some inner visualization, so you would 'see' the dark rain cloud you are not supposed to think about. In many cases the negative image which is conjured up by the words 'dark rain cloud' will affect you subconsciously, regardless of the actual injunction not to think about the subject. Thinking about missing tends to make you miss, and thinking about failing tends to bring failure. Each unconscious 'reminder' of a negative (or 'disempowering') image detracts from the positive goal we are actually aiming for. Parents know what it is to waste their breath telling a child what not to do ('Don't get your shoes dirty', 'Don't spill it'), and wondering whether it would have been better to tell them the very opposite. So it is better to imagine a sunny day and blue skies from the start, if that is what you want. Turn your negative goal into a positive one.

Own part   Try to be sure that your goal can be fulfilled within your reasonable personal control. Consider what will be your 'own part' in achieving your goal. Whether your goal is personal or part of your work, it is important to keep to an absolute minimum the number of potential excuses as to why you might not eventually succeed. One of the most common reasons for failure is other people, departments or functions. It is better to try to get your goals clarified at the outset, rather than find that circumstances outside your control prevent you from achieving what you want.

As with the distinction between positive and negative, this is not always as clear as black or white, and you may have to make a judgement about whether you will have enough control over a situation to really own a goal. In many circumstances you will be part of a team, and the goal will be a team effort. The question then will be whether you have enough influence within the team to make the goal yours (as well as the team's, department's or company's), or whether you cannot justify making it a personal goal. If you are the manager or team leader at work, even though you depend on other people, it is reasonable to make a group goal your own. At very worst, you will be responsible for influencing, persuading and motivating your team and that, of course, is within your power and role. Given the authority, you can acquire the interpersonal skills you need. If, on the other hand, you are just one of a team, you may not have the influence over policy or methods to affect the final outcome one way or another, however skilfully you contribute to the team. The team objective, therefore, does not really meet this 'own part' test.

The same would apply in a leisure context if you are a team member in a sport. Let us assume that your goal is to gain promotion from the third division to the first division in the next two seasons. If you are just a member of the team, and conscientiously play your part in achieving the goal, it would be unreasonable for you to be blamed eventually if the goal were not achieved. However, if you were the team captain or manager, then it would be more reasonable for you to look upon the goal as your own. Although you could not achieve the goal on your own, your role and authority would give you the degree of control that is necessary to qualify as a well-formed outcome.

If you are uncertain as to what your *own part* will be in the achievement of any goal, ask the question: What exactly will *I* do to achieve this goal? If the answer is precious little, it clearly does not rank as a well-formed outcome, as you will have good reason for non-achievement. To fix a goal that has a good chance of success, you must be able and willing to take full personal responsibility for the achievement of that goal, whatever your formal responsibility. If you cannot, then it is better to understand this at the outset. In some cases you may be able to change the situation, obtaining the resources and authority you need. Or you may have to amend your goal so that it passes the 'own part' test. While you may not be able to get the team into the next division single-handed, you can assist by doing something that *is* within your power. As a trainer on a sales training course, for example, you may not be able to increase sales directly, but you may be able to demonstrate that trainees have increased their product knowledge, which will in turn have an indirect effect on sales results.

Specific Make sure that your goals are quite specific. Ask yourself questions that start who, where, when, what and how ... *specifically.* This will further reduce the possibility for excuses. It does help at this stage to write down your goal, and sometimes the very act of expressing it in words makes it clearer and more likely to be achieved.

As far as possible, try to quantify your goals. In many cases, you should also be able to put a date on their achievement. If you have a personal goal to speak a foreign language, for instance, how can you be more specific in expressing this goal? There is a big difference between the level of language you need to scrape through on your two weeks' holiday on the continent, and the level you would need for a real conversation or if you intended to work in an overseas country. While never underestimating the problem of evaluating any training or development intervention, the problems are multiplied when outcomes are not made specific. Even lowering your sights, but being specific (for example, in having a completion date, or criteria for success) is likely to produce greater real outputs—that is, contribute more to outcomes higher up the organization's hierarchy of goals.

Therefore, it is not enough to want to be 'a good, professional trainer', or to 'do well in my career', any more than it is to say you want to be happy. Break your goal down into specific chunks that you can start to do something about. Even to 'run a successful programme' begs the question of how you, and others, will measure success—which introduces another test of a clear goal: the evidence of success.

Evidence   Sometimes it helps if you can determine in advance the acceptable
evidence that you have fulfilled your goal. In the case of the foreign
language, for instance, having decided specifically on the level you
wish to reach, you may be able to translate this into some evidence. If
the level is equivalent to a GCSE 'O' level or 'A' level, and you want to
make this your goal, then the evidence will be the certificate that you
receive when you succeed. This sort of tangible evidence makes it
easier for you and others to know just whether and when a goal has
been achieved. Also, the physical evidence can be *imagined*, or
visualized, and is usually a motivator to keep you pressing towards
achievement.

In many business situations, where results or outputs are in terms of
sales, profits or other financial results, the evidence is usually quite
obvious. The same applies to winning new customers, collecting debts
or getting delegates onto a training course or conference. So, wherever
possible, try to think of appropriate evidence that will support your
outcome. This, of course, is linked with the previous requirement that
your goal is specific. A woolly goal is unlikely to have evidence to
support it, which helps to keep it woolly.

If no evidence would naturally be forthcoming, then you may need to
use some ingenuity to decide on a suitable form of evidence. This will
be as much for your purposes as the goal achiever, proving to the
world, or the organization, that you have achieved your goal. But it
will form a mental target, something that can be readily visualized. In
most cases it is not difficult to decide on evidence. If your goal is to
reach a certain lower (or higher) weight by a certain date, for example,
then the evidence of the bathroom scales is probably all that you need.
If, however, your goal is to be a better driver, you might need to be
more specific about what your goal is, and find out whether there
would be suitable evidence in the form of an advanced driving
certificate that would make your goal more robust. Usually, evidence is
something that can be seen or heard or handled—something that can
be clearly imagined. If you draw a blank on evidence, particularly if your
goal also fails the other tests, you may have to abandon or amend your
goal. In applying the evidence test to your outcome, ask yourself the
question, What will I see, hear and feel when I have it or when I achieve
it, and will I know for definite that I have achieved my goal? Wherever
possible introduce some evidence that supports your specific goals.

Resources   Ask yourself: What resources do I need to get this outcome? In many
cases the resources that you need will be readily obtainable, and part of
your job as the goal achiever will be to marshal those resources. But the
main resource is you, and the innate drive and skills that you possess to
bring about your goal. And this is more to do with physical and mental
resources than money, people, machines and external resources which
you would be able to obtain—if necessary—as interim goals.

When some people fail to achieve the goals they have set for themselves, you may hear others saying 'He didn't have it in him.' In other words, it was unreasonable from the outset for the person to set such a goal. In this sense, we need to check that we have the innate resources to bring about the goal we have in mind. To choose extreme examples, if you do not have the physical build to be a heavyweight boxer or a ballerina, then however specific and positive your goal might be, it would not pass the resources test. Most of us can readily quote examples of people who have achieved outstanding goals against all the odds and despite any lack of physical ability and education, and although we should not underrate ourselves we should also apply some common sense. If your goal is to be a managing director, there probably is not a problem. A quick review of existing managing directors will reveal an enormous range of physical and mental abilities. Quite simply, you don't have to be an Einstein, or a Mohammed Ali, to be a top business manager—or many other things. It is difficult to imagine a person who would *not* have the innate resources to be the leader of a company or an organization. The resources that would be needed to achieve that goal, such as a knowledge of management or perhaps finance, or certain people skills, can all be acquired. The acquisition of those missing resources becomes a new, specific and quite achievable goal in its own right.

All this has great significance in training and development. To have belief in a learning process the learner needs to have some confidence in his or her innate ability to achieve the outcome—be it a level of skill or command of an area of knowledge. A programme director will need to match the resources of trainees—in the sense we are using it—with the demands and outcomes of a programme.

The resources test will also determine what other *acquirable* resources are needed (such as time, funds, an elementary skill, or a level of physical fitness), and how these can be obtained in preparation for greater outcomes.

It is sometimes difficult to determine an individual's innate resource and what he or she can acquire. Because of our tendency to underestimate our potential, a good rule of thumb is to assume we can acquire resources unless we and those who know us well 'just cannot imagine' that we can achieve the outcome in question. Although we use the words unwittingly, this is a matter of fact, and failure to visualize an outcome is a clear indication that the goal is unlikely to be achieved.

Size Is your goal the right size for you? That is: Is it big enough to motivate you and keep you motivated right to its conclusion, or is it too small and not enough to stretch you? If an outcome is too large, it can usually be divided up into smaller parts. We can often manage one phase of a project, or part of something bigger. If, on the other hand, it is too small, you might be able to make the goal bigger, or make it more demanding by giving yourself a tighter timescale. Either way, you need to balance the goal with your resources and experience.

There is a fine balancing line in fixing a goal at the right level. Different people work to different levels of stress and respond differently to different demands. Sometimes we work best when the adrenaline is flowing and the demands of the job seem just slightly beyond us, yet we are challenged to achieve.

If your goal is an organizational one, and you feel you can do something better or more quickly, then give yourself a private goal. Plan to go 'the extra mile', or make your goal an earlier date. You will be able to surprise and impress your managers, and at the same time motivate yourself to do a major, challenging job.

Most of us know the experience of facing a task that is so big that we are not able to even think about it, so we tend to freeze and do nothing, or at least do nothing constructive, until it is too late. To avoid the guilt we busy ourselves with something else—which usually takes the form of effort and activity (inputs) rather than outputs. By fixing the right size of goal at the outset, you can avoid these wheel-spins, which account for so much non-achievement. Conversely, one of the most common causes of non-achievement is the lack of motivation that comes from undertaking a task that is too small. Motivation, of course, is a bigger factor in achieving goals than technical knowledge or specific skills (all of which a motivated person will quickly acquire as necessary). So the size test, while simple to apply, is vital to effectiveness.

Ecology frame   There is one final and important test to apply to your goal. A lot is said nowadays about the environment and ecology. We know that what happens in one part of the world can influence another, however indirectly, and we cannot live our lives in isolation. Something similar applies when seeking to achieve goals. One goal can affect another. A career goal, for example, might well affect domestic and social life, and success in one area might lead to disaster in another. So an ecology check, in the context of your goals or outcomes, means checking to see how one goal might influence another, and thus affect your motivation and the chances of either, or both goals being fulfilled. This usually demands hard decisions on your part. You may have to sort out your priorities—which is the more important goal to achieve—or, more likely, you will have to amend one goal or another, to bring them in line.

But the ecological links in the environment can go a lot further afield than your own immediate surroundings, and your goals might have an effect on other people, just as other people's goals sometimes affect you. So, in doing the ecology check, you should also ask yourself: What impact will my goals have on other people? In some cases, people seek to achieve their outcomes with no reference at all to the people who will be harmed, or adversely affected in the wake of their achievements. In the long run, of course, this usually rebounds on the individual achiever and, just as in the external environment, we pay the price for our short-term indulgence. You should therefore ask yourself: Who else might this affect?, and a simple amendment to your goal might resolve this and even make it better in the long term.

Another simple test to check for ecology is to ask yourself: If I got this (the outcome you are aiming for) straight away, would I take it? This might seem like a silly question, but often we call our own bluff and realize that we are not committed to a goal. Going back to the managing director example, if you could have that goal immediately, would you take it—with all the responsibility, new situations and 'headaches' it entails? If you hesitate, maybe the ecology is not quite right—there might be conflict between your managing director goal and others.

Sometimes it is difficult to identify the other forces that might operate against our achieving our goals. Some of these are unconscious. When setting out to achieve a goal of losing weight, for instance, there are probably other positive intentions that have been keeping us overweight for years. These will come to mind when we start to consider the wider ecology of any individual goal.

Fitting goals together

Having established clear goals it remains to ensure that your goals fit together, lower day-to-day ones supporting higher long-term ones, and that they are all aiming in the same direction. A hierarchy of goals applies personally as well as in an organization. T&D will similarly have to dovetail, eventually contributing to the mission of the organization. An apparently successful training event produces happy, smiling managers at the end, as well as shining written reviews or other forms of evaluation. But these outcomes might not necessarily match a higher objective of relevance to the manager's job, of better performance in that job according to key targets, or to measurable performance at a departmental or strategic business unit level. In terms of inputs and outputs, such evidence might confirm good inputs rather than any quality of output. Achievement of functional objectives, however, would still not constitute business or organizational success if they in turn do not contribute to corporate level goals. The hierarchy is further extended if you consider the outcomes of stakeholders such as shareholders, customers and managers who will indirectly be affected by any training and development objective.

There are major difficulties in goal fixing and performance measurement at each level, and the timescale is one dimension that has to be considered. At the lowest level—for instance, objectives within the training period—timescales are usually short. Significant changes back in the job will no doubt have to be monitored over a longer period. The overall impact of T&D on the whole business might take even longer to evaluate because of the nature of the goals at that level in the hierarchy. The requirements might include various technical skills, more general people or management skills, product and market knowledge, and a general appreciation of business matters such as finance or marketing. The latter, while vital for the success of the business, will not be measurable over a short timescale. At higher outcome levels more people and subjectivity are likely to be involved in policy, financing, and 'politics'. Figure 3.1 illustrates the hierarchy of goals within an organization, from the corporate level down to individual jobs. These may be documented at various levels in the form of a mission statement, corporate and business unit plans and budgets, departmental objectives, individual job descriptions, and personal 'to do' lists. As well as fitting vertically, goals will also have to relate horizontally— between divisions or regions, for example, and particularly between different functions. A training outcome will have to integrate with wider personnel goals, which in turn will form part of the organization's strategic intentions.

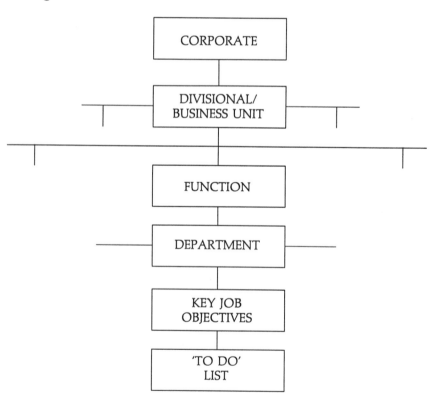

Figure 3.1 *Hierarchy of goals (organization)*

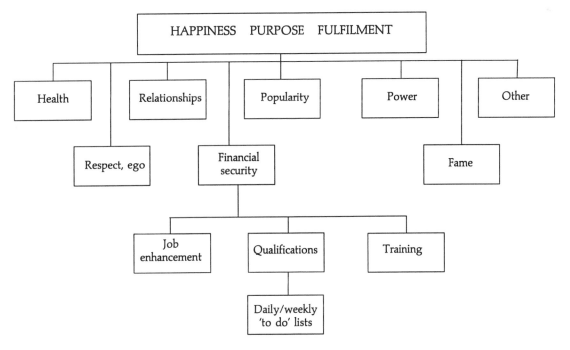

Figure 3.2 *Hierarchy of goals (personal)*

Figure 3.2 illustrates the hierarchy of goals that might apply personally. In this case the hierarchy relates to one person, and it is less likely that goals will have been documented or formalized. It is also likely that some goals will operate below our consciousness—as positive intentions. The different levels and elements, however, are just as interdependent—vertically as well as horizontally. We need to be pulling in the same direction to achieve higher level goals.

The individual trainer or manager operates in both hierarchies, both as a person and as a cog in an organizational machine. Hopefully, the organization's outcomes will be reflected in personal goals—perhaps concerning respect, power or financial security. In practice the link between a company return on investment goal and 'I want to be respected' might be tenuous indeed, so potential personal 'power' is lost to the organization and its stakeholders.

Organizational success depends upon channelling resources and groups of people into achieving the overall outcome or mission. At an individual level this means, to a reasonable extent at least, combining personal and organizational goals. Personal success depends upon channelling one's own resources into achieving an overall 'mission'—the higher goals of contentment, fulfilment or whatever. Personal success within an organization will depend upon the extent to which personal and organizational goals coincide, so that commitment and motivation (a feature of people and not organizations) is harnessed.

An appreciation of both hierarchies will tend to produce better and clearer goals at every level. It will, at worst, show where corporate and personal strategies meet—at the individual clerk, salesperson, trainer or manager—and the true source of quality, excellence and other worthy things that organizations aim for.

Individual and corporate objectives

NLP is mainly concerned with the individual, but so should the organization at every turn. The connection, for instance through the training function, is not difficult to make.

Some of the principles and techniques of NLP are applicable at a personal rather than corporate level. Rapport, for example, which is crucial for communication within organizations, happens between individual people. Its effect, therefore, on the organization is on a *group of people*. Similarly a motivated workforce is a lot of individually motivated people. Whatever the group synergies at work, or economies of scale, the organization relies upon its component parts, the individuals. From my own experience as a trainer and businessman I have extended the simple feedback cycle for goal achievement right up to a corporate level. But the corporation, or institution, is always a collection of individuals. As a legal, soulless entity it cannot have goals or dreams. There is, however, another link between the individual and the organization. From my work with top business leaders it can be shown that missions and strategies can often be traced to the vision of a leader—an individual. So what appears a distant corporate goal at lower levels in the organization might be a clear and very personal dream or vision on the part of an individual entrepreneur, CEO or managing director, subject to all the principles and techniques of NLP. Because the human mind is the supreme model of excellence, and NLP is the study of human excellence, organizational systems and structures can benefit from the goal-achievement principles that work at a personal level.

So any goal-directed behaviour, first at an individual level and by logical extension at a group or organizational level, tends to fit the four-stage success model we met in Chapter 2. Decide what you want or where you want to be; do what you think is best to achieve this goal; notice carefully how you are doing; and be ready to change what you are doing if something does not work. In your own organization, the change will have to start with you.

4 The structure of thought

The presuppositions of NLP make it clear that in order to understand our behaviour and the behaviour of others we must at least begin to understand how we think. The different maps each of us has are different ways of thinking. A desire, or 'positive intention' that accounts for a person's behaviour involves thought processes, whether conscious or unconscious. And thought precedes behaviour.

The neuro part of neuro-linguistic programming makes this association with the brain. Similarly, we can hardly discuss language—the linguistic part—without considering how we think. Language is usually considered a special feature of human cognition, and when thinking about abstract things in particular, it is difficult to imagine what we would do without the use of words and language.

NLP has managed to simplify the way we think into a model, with a standard language, so that we can communicate about highly subjective thought processes. This form of thought modelling is one of the aspects of NLP that allows it to develop with some scientific credibility, even though the subjective nature of what is being studied is well outside what existing scientific laws can accommodate. An understanding of thought processes will advance our understanding and practice of human communication, and what we might call human excellence.

Unconscious thinking

In some cases ordinary language is adequate to describe thinking processes. If you set students a problem then ask them how they arrived at their answers—i.e. what their thought processes were—you will probably get satisfactory answers about how they think. They might explain the logic behind what they did, and the series of steps they took to arrive at a mathematical solution or some verbal reasoning. Highly *conscious* thought processes can be described—if not fully explained—to some degree at least. Conscious, left-brain thinking is in any event language based, so it is the part of our thinking that can be communicated. In some forms of thinking, however, you are not so clear about how you 'thought', or whether you thought at all—for example, in explaining why you behaved in a particular way. In some cases you might not be personally aware of a positive intention—a purpose or reason—that brings about some behaviour. The thinking is unconscious.

But unconscious thinking applies in other situations. We are, it seems, thinking all the time, or at least performing some mental operations that result in behaviour, yet clearly we do not consciously think about more than one thing at a time. If, when driving a car, you take a particular action that someone else notices and asks 'Why did you do that?', you may not even have been aware of what you were doing. We drive, and do a hundred other everyday things, without thinking consciously about what we are doing. If we did we would probably make a mess of any automatic kind of job. Hardly anyone is aware at the time of which sock they put on first, or which side of their face they shave first, let alone why. Yet these behaviours are subject to sophisticated control from the brain.

Dr Emile Donchin, at the Champaign-Urbana University of Illinois, says that more than 99 per cent of all learning, for example, is non-conscious. Other researchers argue that over 90 per cent of all our thinking is below consciousness, and that we are just aware of the tip of an iceberg. So we need to understand what the brain is doing most of the time, sometimes involving the most complex of tasks. The cases I have mentioned refer to the many behaviours which, through habit, have become automatic. If you try to think of more examples, starting from when you get up in the morning, you should easily fill a sheet of paper.

Autopilot This unconscious mode of thought seems to be the secret in all sorts of feats of excellence. The moment you think consciously about doing something that should really be automatic, your performance drops. If your car passenger is an expert driver who you think might be critical, your standard of performance, despite all your attention, paradoxically falls. In other words, the harder you try, the worse you get.

The more activities you can relegate to this category of unconscious thought, or 'autopilot', the more effective you will be. You perform all sorts of skills better in this mode. When you consider that some people do amazing feats in just this way—from giving a public speech to winning at championship tennis, or running a company—the potential becomes clear. So thinking—of one kind or another—is the basis of all our behaviour, and conscious thought is just the tip of the iceberg. NLP allows us to understand and start to control these below-the-surface thoughts. This is fundamental to skills training.

Thoughts that rise to the surface But unconscious thinking is not confined to managing these previously learned functions. If you are discussing an old friend over dinner, you may be able to visualize the person's face, but not remember his or her name. There are two approaches you can adopt. You can try hard to remember the name, perhaps using some mental system you have devised, such as working through the alphabet. The chances are, however, that you will be lying awake in the early hours of the following morning still trying to remember the name. The other approach is not to care—'Never mind, it'll come to me in a minute.' (It does not really matter in any case, it was the annoyance at not being able to remember quickly that spurred on the hard thinking in the first approach.) A few minutes later, in the middle of some other topic of conversation, the name floats into your memory as a gift from the gods.

This is different from the brain process that enables you to clean your teeth, cut up your food, or carry empty cups into the kitchen—the co-ordination of physical activities. You are addressing a problem, resorting to memory—you are *thinking*. But, having 'instructed' your problem, or outcome, the job is done below your consciousness, and it certainly seems, in this case, that this kind of thinking is much more efficient than the conscious kind. If you have ever woken up in the night with a bright idea, or solution to some pressing problem, you will appreciate the power and value of this sort of thinking, which carries on while you are asleep, so can be a great help in time management. Although conspicuously absent from conventional learning and training models, this part of our thinking is also a fundamental part of achieving outcomes.

How you think

A lot of research has been carried out in recent years on understanding how the human brain works. In one sense it might be expected that any scientific quest will eventually concentrate on the most complex bit of life—by a very long way—that we know of. But developments in other areas of science have made the present work more feasible. Computing developments, for instance, in various kinds of brain scanning, allow us to record, in effect, the very process of thought (including unconscious thought) while, however, being light years away from recording the content of those thoughts. The shift away from a behaviourist approach to psychology, which relied on observable behaviour, to a cognitive approach, which recognizes the importance of the subjective thought processes themselves in explaining behaviour, has also had a positive effect. Some argue that the behaviourist epoch actually delayed progress in our understanding of the mind. Similar claims have been made about the limiting analogy between digital computers and the human brain, which we now know is in an altogether different league. The more recent 'lifespan' approach to cognitive psychology, which considers the way our thinking changes throughout life (although earlier work had given plenty of attention to child development, ending the development of cognition during teenage years) has also give a more dynamic basis to our approach to the human mind. The Nobel prize winning research of Roger Sperry in the 1960s involving split-brain experiments gave a quantum impetus to our understanding of how the two sides of the brain, right and left, are involved in different kinds of thought processes. This right–left distinction is one of the major advances in our understanding of how we think, and not surprisingly has influenced more recent developments in applied psychology such as NLP.

Two sides of the brain

Roger Sperry's work involved experiments on patients in whom the corpus callosum, the bundle of nerve fibres which join the right and left sides of the brain (specifically the hemispheres of the cortex, or upper brain) had been severed, mainly to prevent serious epileptic seizures from spreading to the other side of the brain. Although we already had a lot of understanding about the specialization of each side of the brain, the experiments had been almost wholly restricted to animals (due to a shortage of human volunteers!). Sperry's work confirmed much of what had been assumed, but advanced our knowledge further, including, for instance, the significance of right- and left-handedness. The more recent use of scanning technology has allowed us to apply ever more sophisticated tests to normal humans, so there is now an irrefutable body of knowledge about what is termed *hemispherical specialization*— the respective roles of the right and left sides of the upper brain. While NLP cannot be linked directly with these developments in the fields of neurology and physiology, it has been more readily accepted in the context of all the contemporary scientific work on the human brain and the mind. The idea of hemispherical specialization, however, is central to any study of learning and training.

My earlier book, *The Right Brain Manager* (Piatkus), described this right–left brain distinction, and how an understanding of it helps in all sorts of activities, such as memory and controlling how we feel. Here I shall give just a brief overview, although it will be discussed as each NLP topic is presented.

Left-brain logic

The left brain controls all physical movement on the right side of the body, and the right side of the brain controls all movement on the left side. As far as this motor function is concerned, both sides of the brain do essentially the same basic job. These, of course, are not conscious brain processes. If you decide to get out of your chair, hundreds of sophisticated muscular and chemical changes happen without effort. But higher level thought has become specialized to some degree, so that verbal and language processing, and logical or sequential reasoning, take place primarily in the left brain. As far as language is concerned, this is very pronounced, and a vast amount of research has proved this. So a brain seizure or stroke affecting the left side of the brain (affecting the right side of the body) will invariably result in speech impediment. External damage to the left side will similarly impair speech, but if this happens at an early age the brain is able to compensate, and the other side slowly learns new skills.

Right-brain creativity

The right side of the brain is adept at spatial tasks, creative activities, and music and art. It works holistically—as a whole—rather than breaking things into component parts to understand them, or working through a problem in sequential steps. So a stroke victim with damage to the right side of the brain will not suffer a speech loss, but might be disoriented spatially—even getting lost when going from one room to another. This holistic way of seeing things allows the right brain, for instance, to recognize a face from many years ago even though there are many individual changes (such as a beard or glasses) that would confuse the left brain. Thus, on entering a crowded room you might instantly feel that you have seen a person before, even though his or her name—and anything else you might want to express in words—eludes you. Although this kind of thinking is uncannily quick, and is sometimes associated with 'first impressions' about people, it might not be expressible in words. Thus you might feel 'right' about a person, based on what might be called positive chemistry, even though your judgement is not based on a reasoned thought process, and your feeling is not readily expressible in language.

The brain partnership

In combination, these entirely different modes of thinking are a formidable duo, and account for human excellence in any area. Where we see both sides working fully, such as the wild imagination and cold logic of an Einstein, we witness what is termed genius. The early work on the brain hemispheres concentrated on the functions each side performed best, such as language and maths on the left, and art, music and creative thought on the right. It is now clear that the distinction is more the result of the way thoughts are processed, rather than the function or content of the thought. Sometimes art and music, for example, will engage the logical left brain when structure is important, while the scientist may occasionally use his right brain for creative leaps of imagination. In practice, we require both sides of the brain to carry out any reasonably complex task with excellence. Sadly, the right brain is often suppressed or even atrophies in an environment of learning that is based entirely on logic and structure. Most organizational training follows the pattern of left-brain thinking.

Software and hardware

As 'hardware', both sides of the brain are (for practical purposes) the same. The difference is in the way they are used—that is, in the different programmes of thought. There is no explanation as to why the language specialization is so strong, or why it happens to 'choose' the left side. We do know that a slight bias in early childhood (for parents, about the time that you are not sure whether your child is right-handed or left-handed) is amplified as each side literally specializes in what it can do best. Technically, the specialization could have gone the other way, as applies to a small proportion of the population (nearly all of them left-handed) whose brain functions work the other way round. This heavy brain hemisphere skewing is directly linked to handedness.

More than 95 per cent of right-handers follow the left-brain language pattern (or dominance), and the rest are reversed. Some 70 per cent of left-handers follow the same pattern (i.e. left-brain dominance), and of the remainder about 15 per cent use the reverse side (i.e. right brain for language) while the other 15 per cent are fully bicameral—that is, there is no specialization at one side or the other. So, apart from a small percentage of the total population (15 per cent of left-handers) left-brain dominance seems to apply. Moreover, it appears that left-brain dominance is even more marked among managers and professionals such as trainers, and those who have had a 'good' education.

Representation systems

What do we mean by thinking? We are aware of the world through our five senses: seeing, hearing, feeling, tasting and smelling. From descriptions of conscious thought processes it quickly becomes apparent that these representation systems are used internally when we remember, consider, ponder, etc.—in other words, when we think. Most people are able to visualize a scene internally, either recalling a memory or imagining a future event. Similarly we can recall sounds, such as the spoken word, and project our thoughts into the future to imagine a sound. When recalling a particularly pleasant or unpleasant event in which we also had strong feelings, we are very likely to recall the feelings as well as the event. It is a 'package' of all five ways of experiencing the world around. So as well as being able to represent each of the senses inwardly—such as imagining picking up fresh snow to make a snowball—this internal system also accounts for what we call our state of mind, or how we feel. The total 'experience' thus has its own characteristics, evoking happiness, fear, calmness, or any other state.

Seeing is the most common sense we use in thinking, followed by hearing, then feeling. Tasting and smelling can also be represented inwardly, although it seems they are used far less in everyday thought processing. These main three 'representation systems' account for all our 'thinking', and form a model that allows us to describe, understand, and use the processes for particular purposes.

Getting to know your thought modalities

You can try out any of these thinking systems yourself. Start with a memory—choose a particular event in the past, preferably one that is easily recalled and quite vivid. Visualize the sights as clearly as you can, then concentrate on the sounds separately, then the feelings. If you imagine lying on a beach, for instance, you might feel the sand or towel, and the warmth of the sun on your body, hear the screeching gulls, and see the swaying branches of the trees. Then bring these together and re-live the total experience, making it as real as you can. You can also experience the emotion of the occasion by conjuring up exactly how you felt.

Incidentally, while you are doing this all your actual body indicators will change—your blood pressure, the chemical balance of the body, etc., to reflect your state of mind and accompanying physical characteristics at the time you are recalling. You might want to try tasting and smelling, but do not worry if these are not so easy to recall.

You can do the same exercise at the present time: for example, picturing your child at school, or your partner at work. As well as bridging time by memory, you can also span distances, hearing the sound of a village church bell ringing hundreds of miles away, or feeling the rocks at your favourite holiday beach. You can also project your thoughts into the future. In this case you can either imagine a future actual event, such as the forthcoming school play or an important training session you have to conduct, or you can create something from nothing. In the latter case your brain cleverly synthesizes something you have never directly experienced inwardly or outwardly. Imagine, for instance, seeing your house in the middle of a field a few miles away. Give it a bright blue roof. Then change the curtains. The mind is able to represent apparently new thoughts, although in fact it draws from what you have experienced (like a house, or 'blue') from your memory data bank, including every book you have read and every television programme you have watched.

In each of these cases you used your representation systems, the inner equivalent of the outward senses, to do the thinking. Your description of those thoughts will be in the same terms as a description of the view outside your window, or the room in which you are sitting. To the brain, where colours and tastes are experienced, it seems there is no distinction.

Identifying submodalities
We have, therefore, visual, auditory and kinaesthetic (feeling) representation systems, as well as gustatory (taste) and olfactory (smell) senses which are less used in everyday thought processing. Any memory or imagined event can be broken into these constituent parts and described, just as we might describe a real experience. But the model goes a lot further. A visual image, for instance, might be very clear or unfocused, in black and white or full colour, close or distant, still or moving—much as we might describe the picture on our television screen. These characteristics of the visual representation system, or visual modality, are termed *submodalities*. They allow us to describe thought processes otherwise too subjective to communicate. Sounds might similarly be quiet or loud, high or low frequency, staccato or legato. A spoken voice might be deep and resonant or high pitched and staccato, and so on. The sound might seem to come from the front, from behind, or be all round. A kinaesthetic feeling similarly might be hot or cold, rough or smooth, soft or hard, and any of the various characteristics we might use to describe a physical feeling. We sometimes talk of an overall feeling 'in the pit of the stomach', or refer to a 'sinking feeling', or of being elated or depressed.

Thus any account of thoughts—memories or imagination—will be in the form of representation systems and their submodalities. While still very subjective, they can at least be expressed in a common NLP language of communication.

Examples of submodalities in each of the three main representation systems, or modalities, are listed in Table 4.1.

Table 4.1   *Modalities and submodalities*

Modality	Submodality	
Visual	Brightness	Contrast
	Size	Clarity
	Colour/black and white	Focus
	Saturation (vividness)	Framed/panoramic
	Hue or colour balance	Movement
	Shape	Perspective
	Location	Associated/dissociated
	Distance	3-Dimensional/flat
Auditory	Pitch	Duration
	Tempo (speed)	Location
	Volume	Distance
	Rhythm	External/internal
	Continuous/interrupted	Source
	Timbre or tonality	Mono/stereo
	Digital (words)	Clarity
	Associated/dissociated	Number
Kinaesthetic (sensations)	Pressure	Movement
	Location	Duration
	Number	Intensity
	Texture	Shape
	Temperature	Frequency (tempo)

Sensory preference

Whatever the complexity of the neural process in a thought activity, we have a communication vehicle we can use in the form of representation systems. It quickly becomes apparent that some people are quite at home when describing such thoughts, and others find it difficult, if not impossible. It is much more common, however, that a person will be happy with, say, visualizing—seeing pictures inwardly and describing these in terms of various submodalities—but finds it difficult to conjure up sounds, or vice versa. Or a person might be much more at home recalling feelings than visual images. This is termed *sensory preference*—quite simply, the individual's preference to use one inner sense rather than another. Such a preference might well reflect an outward sensory preference. One person notices sights more than sounds, for example. Sometimes this is accentuated by the sort of work a person does, which might require special acuity in observing or listening—or for that matter the sense of touch. But a person's inward sensory preference does not necessarily reflect an outward preference or ability.

Establishing sensory rapport

The idea of sensory preference is an important contribution of NLP, and has enormous significance in training and development. It has been found, for example, that people with a similar preference get along well together, experiencing good rapport. They may not be aware of *why* the rapport exists, and other personality factors such as introversion or extroversion, for instance, or indeed beliefs or political affiliation, do not account for the apparent mutual liking. Conversely, a serious lack of rapport occurs when people of different sensory preferences try to communicate. Each of us usually has a preference in the way we 'represent' our world—in the way we think. This, in turn, affects our behaviour, not least in our relationship with others who do not think in the same way, but also the kind of work we like, how we buy, how we learn, and the kind of training we respond to.

This confirms the idea of our individual maps of reality and is another major factor in our unique perception. Although we have the same basic brain with which to process what we are experiencing in the world, any preference, or bias, will inevitably result in different interpretations— different maps. Do you *see* that? Does it *sound* right? Do you *feel* you can apply it in some way?

Allowing for thinking preference

The effect of all this on interpersonal communication will be readily apparent, as will the impact on any form of training and development. Received wisdom argues the power of a visual image in training presentations—hence the use of tools such as overhead projectors and videos. It has been shown that a person with a strong auditory and low visual preference will not respond to even the most professionally produced colour graphics. Another person with a kinaesthetic preference will be more influenced by feeling something—perhaps passing around a product sample that he or she can physically handle— than any combination of sights and sounds. Based on the fact of sensory preference, compromise must apply when we communicate in a group situation, as individuals are likely to have different sensory preferences.

An understanding of sensory preference allows us to design communication processes, whether at an individual or group level, in a more meaningful way, taking account of the representation systems NLP identifies, and the preferences from person to person. We know, for example, that the visual modality is the most used, so it makes sense in a group situation to rank visual images ahead of auditory ones. By careful design of a training activity we should seek to give a choice of modality on a more or less continuous basis, rather than sharing out the visual, auditory and kinaesthetic components of a presentation on a rationed basis. NLP does not come with a set of off-the-shelf techniques for the trainer. It offers, however, some very commonsense principles that are becoming more and more robust as they are applied in different areas, and a thinking model that can be used with a bit of creativity in almost any area of human behaviour. As the biggest impact of NLP is in the field of interpersonal communication, training and development is set to benefit more than most other issues.

Determining someone's thinking preference

You may be aware that you have a thinking preference; for instance, that you prefer to think in pictures, and can easily visualize a situation. Or you may not be sure. Let us first of all determine how we can recognize the thinking preferences of others, then come back to being sure of our own preference.

Predicates

First of all there are clues in what people say, and this is an easy way to establish preference. You might have heard people use these expressions:

> I get the picture.
> That looks clear.
> I see what you mean.

These are expressions, or *predicates*, that indicate a visual preference. Usually a person is not aware they are using such figures of speech, sometimes very frequently throughout the day, but they nevertheless indicate a way of thinking. They are in effect describing just what is happening as they see things. Similarly, you have heard the following:

> That sounds OK.
> I hear what you say.
> I'm listening.
> That rings a bell.
> He turned a deaf ear.

And so on. You can probably think of similar expressions that have an auditory connotation. These indicate a preference for auditory thinking. A person who uses such expressions regularly will probably find it easier to recollect sounds rather than visual images. Such individuals are usually good listeners.

What about these?

> She got a warm response.
> Hold on a minute.
> Did you grasp that point?
> I'll be keeping in touch.

These suggest a kinaesthetic preference. In fact you are likely to hear a whole range of figures of speech, including those linked with tasting and smelling, as these are all part of our everyday language. But a predominance of one kind of predicate usually indicates a sensory preference for that modality, or representation system. There is also evidence from what a person writes. Find a report written by someone in the office and read it carefully, noting any sensory predicates and putting them in the three main categories. You will soon see (notice the visual predicate—I could have said 'You will soon get a feel for ...') any preference.

Non-verbal cues   Another set of cues are non-verbal. A visualizing person tends to speak quickly, usually with a higher pitch than an auditory person, who uses a more resonant tone and speaks more slowly and rhythmically. Images happen very quickly to the visualizing person, and words have difficulty keeping pace. The listening person might adopt a listening posture, with the head a little tilted, almost as though speaking into a telephone, and might also adopt rhythmic body movements such as rocking a foot or tapping a pencil. The kinaesthetic person is altogether slower in verbal responses, taking time to 'feel' their response to a question, often looking down when pondering an answer. A visual person can find it very annoying to converse with a kinaesthetic person, wondering why he or she takes so long to reply and seems to drag everything out. This, of course, explains the lack of rapport that the mismatch produces. And similar mismatching occurs wherever two people with a strong, differing sensory preference try to communicate at the simplest level.

Eye access cues   The third means of establishing sensory preference is the movement of the eyes (Figure 4.1). We have heard for centuries about the eye being the window on the soul, and developments in this field of study have confirmed this in a remarkable way. When we are not conscious of what our eyes are doing (which is more or less all the time, unless we happen to be reading an NLP book) we have a tendency to direct them in certain directions when undertaking thinking tasks such as remembering or imagining. We tend to look upwards when visualizing, to the left when remembering, and to the right when constructing, as when earlier you saw your house in a field miles away. Or sometimes we stare straight forward, but defocused. When thinking in sounds, eye movements are usually horizontally to the left or right, as if directed to either ear. Again, memory recall is to the left (for example, when recalling the sound of a voice some years ago) and to the right when constructed (for example, when imagining the sound of a piano tumbling down a hillside). Another form of thinking is internal dialogue, where you hold an inner conversation with yourself, or give praise or reprimand. Internal dialogue is usually accompanied by eye movements down and to the left. Finally, feelings and bodily sensations are usually accompanied by eye movements down and to the right.

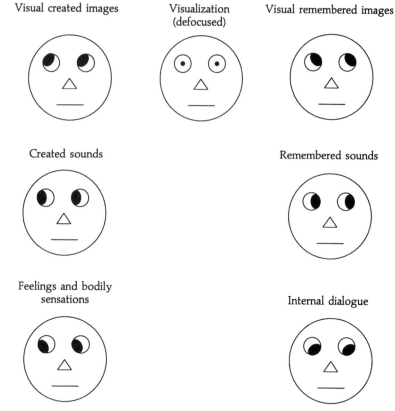

Figure 4.1 *Eye access cues*

These so-called eye access cues provide another way in which you can determine a person's thinking preference. Two or three questions that require deliberation, for instance, might result in a similar pattern of eye movement, suggesting visual, auditory or kinaesthetic dominance. It takes some practice to spot this, as eye movements tend to be rapid. And in most cases we use more than one representation system, so a single thought can involve a whole pattern of internal experiencing—pictures, sounds and feelings—all reflected in eye movements. If no dominant eye pattern is observed, the person probably does not have a particularly dominant thinking preference.

Determining your own sensory preference

It remains to determine your own preference, if you are not already aware of it. The eye movements are not much help unless you can enlist the aid of a friend or relative, but it is important that they test you when you are not aware of what is happening. Although it is difficult not to move your eyes when in thinking mode, I have learned from conducting many seminars that it is possible with a lot of concentration to prevent normal eye movements. You may also have difficulty in monitoring the predicates you use, as, again, we all use these expressions without thinking although you can certainly go through a report or some other document you have written to see if any pattern emerges. But why not try a simple exercise to measure your preference subjectively? In Table 4.2 I have listed a few exercises taken from my book *NLP: The New Art and Science of Getting What You Want*. All you have to do is assess how easy or difficult it is for you to make an inner visual, auditory or kinaesthetic representation. For instance, if a thought is very clear and focused—almost as real as real life—you should score high on the subjective score chart. I have used the scale of 1 to 9, so in the case just mentioned you would give yourself 9. If you have difficulty getting any clear image, or it is transient, a score of 1 or 2 is more appropriate. If you are honest and consistent in your instinctive scoring, you will finish up with your likely preference.

Table 4.2 *Determining your sensory preference*

Visual

1 Which of your friends or relatives has the longest hair?   1 2 3 4 5 6 7 8 9
2 Recall the face of a teacher from when you were at school.   1 2 3 4 5 6 7 8 9
3 Visualize the stripes on a tiger.   1 2 3 4 5 6 7 8 9
4 See the colour of the front door where you live or work.   1 2 3 4 5 6 7 8 9
5 See a favourite entertainer wearing a top hat on your TV screen.   1 2 3 4 5 6 7 8 9
6 Visualize the largest book in your house.   1 2 3 4 5 6 7 8 9

Auditory

1 Hear a favourite tune.   1 2 3 4 5 6 7 8 9
2 Listen to church bells ringing in the distance.   1 2 3 4 5 6 7 8 9
3 Which of your friends has the quietest voice?   1 2 3 4 5 6 7 8 9
4 Hear a car engine starting on a cold morning.   1 2 3 4 5 6 7 8 9
5 Imagine hearing the voice of a childhood friend.   1 2 3 4 5 6 7 8 9
6 Listen to the sound your voice makes under water.   1 2 3 4 5 6 7 8 9

Kinaesthetic

1 Feel your left hand in very cold water.   1 2 3 4 5 6 7 8 9
2 Hold a smooth, glass paperweight in both hands.   1 2 3 4 5 6 7 8 9
3 Stroke a cat or dog.   1 2 3 4 5 6 7 8 9
4 Put on a pair of wet socks.   1 2 3 4 5 6 7 8 9
5 Imagine jumping off a four-foot-high wall.   1 2 3 4 5 6 7 8 9
6 Roll a car wheel down the road.   1 2 3 4 5 6 7 8 9

Now add up your score in each modality and divide by six to find your average for each one. Notice whether one of the three categories gives you a higher score than the other two, or whether one is significantly lower than the other two. If you want to make your preference score more accurate—although it is just a subjective measure—think of some other examples yourself. You might also want to break down the scoring into memory (recalling) and more imaginative (constructive) thoughts.

If you find you have no particular preference but your scores are generally low, then practice will help just as with any physical skill, and will prove useful in later exercises that will be of specific benefit in controlling feelings and achieving your outcomes. If, on the other hand, your scores are all high, you have a good foundation upon which to base a whole range of mental exercises that can improve your performance in any area you wish. If one or two modalities score lower than the others—that is, you do establish a preference—then you can use this understanding to help you achieve rapport with others. At the very worst, your new knowledge about yourself should make you more aware of differences from person to person, and where vital rapport might be lacking.

When all representation systems are strongly developed and combined, this is known as *synaesthesia*, and is a feature, for example, of those with outstanding memories. Practice at thought processing, and particularly in recognizing distinctions between submodalities in different memories and visualizations, will also provide the skills that will enable you to change your feelings and limiting beliefs. Therefore, it will be beneficial to work through the various exercises in the book as you meet them.

Conclusion

We have seen that the language of the inner senses provides a simple model for understanding and manipulating thought processes. The key personal factors in learning and motivation are based on these thought processes. The model allows us to identify a thinking preference both personally and in the case of other people. And this thinking preference is a fundamental factor in the all-important rapport upon which effective communication depends.

5 Effective communication

We have seen the importance of setting clear goals, and communication is also concerned with achieving outcomes—achieving what we want. Although our communication might be to give information rather than receive or achieve something, we nevertheless have an outcome in mind—perhaps to impress, warn, persuade, or entertain, for example. The measure of our success will therefore be the extent to which we achieve these various objectives. The 'communication' is simply a means to that end. If we overemphasize the means we might lose sight of the outcome, and think in terms of inputs rather than outputs. This is embraced in the presupposition we met in Chapter 2, that the meaning of a communication is the response it produces.

We also looked earlier at our sensory preference, and how we like to relate to the world and other people in terms of what we see, hear and feel. Although our individual maps seek to build up a personal picture of outside reality, some of the biggest problems we ever face are not to do with reality, but with other people's perceptual maps. So an understanding of these models of thinking really comes into its own in the whole area of interpersonal communication. Rapport, in communication, is worth a whole portfolio of systems and techniques and aids. A parallel goal, therefore, in any communication, will be to establish and use rapport.

One of the most common features of successful people is their skill at habitually reaching their goals. They do this by the cycle we first met of fixing a goal, doing something, observing carefully what happens, then changing their behaviour until they get what they want. Good communication, also a feature of successful people, follows the same model. It starts with an outcome and depends upon sensory acuity, feedback and flexibility of behaviour. Good communicators have the knack of getting to the heart of information quickly, and the ability of passing their understanding on just as clearly to others. This, I have noticed, is also a major factor in top leaders. They also seem to be able to differentiate between important information and what is not essential. Thus it seems they can get to the core of an issue, or have 'insight'—they are masters at communication.

Language, and any other component of communication, takes place at different levels. Most of the time we communicate at a surface level, and do not get down to the details. This, of course, is fine for most conversation. But to elicit real understanding we need to be more specific, and this is where our communication tools, such as the Meta Model (Chapter 11), Sleight of Mouth (Chapter 6) and others become helpful. Therefore, the key principles of NLP, such as 'the map is not the territory', form a strong foundation for effective communication—indeed they confirm that communication is central to almost all our behaviour. The various techniques we have met translate the principles into practical behaviour and results.

The map analogy is a humbling one, and underlines the fact that none of us can really know 'reality'. Every individual perceptive map of the world differs. We know from personal experience and anecdote how dramatically one person's understanding can be different from another's. So in communicating, either in words, gestures or overall body language, we are seeking to get nearer to the 'territory' of reality, but, more practically, we are trying to bridge the gap between our map of what is real and the map of the other person. Consequently, congruence between maps, or perceptions, and the transfer of understanding, rather than the futile quest for 'reality', is our objective. And this is how we need to approach communication.

Most of us will readily remember occasions when individual words or gestures were powerful in communicating. A single word, or even a short silence, can convey enormous meaning. You will also remember times when words seemed to be of no avail—you thought you were 'saying' one thing, but the other person received a completely different message. Language is powerful enough to take us towards a goal or away from it. When we learn to use language well, and back it up with our physiology to give congruence, we have begun to communicate in an effective way. The measure of our success is not in the 'telling' or discharging of some 'message'—whether spoken or unspoken—but in achieving whatever is the purpose of the communication.

Asking for what you want

The obvious way to get what you want is, of course, to ask. And here again we find one of the secrets of achievers is that somehow they are able to ask in a way that ensures they get what they want.

Be specific

The first rule in getting what you want through communication is thus to ask specifically, which takes us back to one of the rules of goal clarification—to know exactly what you want.

Can they deliver?

Another rule is to ask someone who can help. Has the person the resources to help you bring about your goal? In our earlier goal clarification tests, resources formed an important part of success; but particularly resources that are personal or innate, that we would need to bring about our own goals. When you resort to other people a similar principle applies and you need to be sure that they have the resources to provide what you need. In effect you are transferring a goal to someone else—your goal, or part of it, becomes their goal. So the same tests of a clear goal apply. The person may not want to help you, but to a large extent persuasion is within your power—you set out by your communication to change their perception. But however skilful a communicator you are, you may not be able to create in the other person the resources they need to fulfil your needs. Therefore, in addition to being specific, check that the person is in a position to help.

What happens Knowing who is able to help requires the skill of sensory acuity we met earlier, in which we watch what happens and learn from hard experience. Most of us know people who are much more reliable than others, and somehow tend to achieve their objective while others are still discussing it. You need to recognize such people, and communicate with them when you want to achieve goals that are outside your own resources.

What's in it for them? You need to make sure there is some benefit for those you approach. What value would they gain by meeting your request or helping you? We know, of course, that people are motivated by very different things, and this again relates to their individual maps of the world. In most cases this personal 'hot button' can be pressed without money or any material reward, by simply appealing to the deeper values or ego of the person. The fourth rule is that your asking communication needs to match your belief. There has to be congruence between what you expect and what you do. There is no room for ambivalence in effective communication. If you are not clear about what you want (that is, you the communicator) and believe that there is only a faint chance of getting it, there is little hope that the communicatee will respond enthusiastically. This belief and focus comes right back to the need to always have a clear goal about what you want. The more clearly your goal has been visualized internally, the stronger will be your belief and expectancy that it will actually materialize.

Keep asking, in different ways The final tip is to ask and ask again until you get what you want. This involves the same cybernetic principle that applies to all goal achievement. You continue to move relentlessly towards a goal even when, for the moment, you seem to be failing. But repeated 'asking' doesn't mean you should ask in exactly the same way. NLP never argues that you should try to do the same thing repeatedly. Instead use your sensory acuity to spot what happens on your first request, and have the flexibility to change your approach until you are successful. With courtesy and ingenuity it is possible to approach the same person to achieve the same goal several times. It is unlikely that the person will be aware of just what is happening, and if he or she realizes, you will tend to be respected for your persistence.

One of the most difficult parts of the communication process is to be specific about what you want. From the Meta Model patterns in Chapter 11 you will see how many of these are concerned with generalizations and assumptions as this is the very sort of language we all use all the time, and yet it repeatedly fails as good communication. At the very worst, precise language will tend to get a quicker and clearer response, so that you do not waste unnecessary time on communication that is not bringing results. So always set any communication in the context of goals and objectives, and always seek for clarity in those goals. Keep asking what are called outcome questions:

- What is my objective?
- What exactly do I want?
- What am I here for?
- What do I want for myself?
- What do I want for you or another party?

You maintain this goal perspective by constantly and habitually asking such questions. Do not spend too much time on *why* questions, because sometimes you will get long subjective justifications and excuses, but very little factual information. Asking someone 'Why didn't you get that training contract?', for example, will probably produce an answer— maybe a long and rational one—but is unlikely to achieve your or your organization's goals. A better question might be *how* the person can change what he or she is doing to improve the chances of getting the next contract. Without sounding facetious, what you really want to know is what exactly the person did to bring about the outcome (losing the contract). Something in the answer will be the key to what to do differently, and to getting it right next time. So *how* and *what* questions are usually more effective than *why* questions.

Mirroring

A lot of attention has been paid in recent years to body language in communication. We know that the actual words we say represent a very small part of the total communication. How we say things—the tone of voice and inflections—are just as important as what we say. Also important is the body language that supports whatever we say— our gestures, and even the most intricate physical movements.

The research shows that when we *mirror* or copy the physiology of the person with whom we are communicating, this creates rapport. In very simple terms, people *like you more* if you act like they do. If you watch people engaged in deep conversation, perhaps on the corner of a street or in an office, it is sometimes amusing to see how their silhouettes or physical profiles mirror each other. They might both be leaning forward with clasped hands, or sitting backwards with their hands behind their heads, for example. This mirroring of posture is an entirely unconscious behaviour, but certainly improves rapport, and thus the effectiveness of any communication.

Although usually carried out unconsciously, you can use mirroring as a positive technique in communication. This includes matching the speed of speech, and whether it is high- or low-pitched, as well as overall body posture, breathing and so on. We saw earlier that our sensory preference—that is, our preference for seeing, hearing and feeling— affects our physiology, so our body language tends to betray our preference. We also found that people with the same thinking preference tend to be compatible, so mirroring is important in creating rapport.

When using the mirroring technique it should not be so obvious as to make the other person aware of what you are doing. Yet, quite amazingly, another person can mirror our physiology very closely, and because we are engaged in the subject of communication and not the process, we are not aware at the time of this matching of body language. So provided you avoid obvious and strange mannerisms and ensure that your mirroring does not immediately follow each and every change of posture, but that you gradually adopt the other person's physiology in a natural, unaffected way, everything will be fine.

Mirroring is more than just mechanical copying. By taking on some of another person's characteristics, in a sense you are getting inside that person's mind, and beginning to understand his or her personal map of reality. Remember that our physiology affects how we feel, so by matching someone else's physical characteristics we adopt, to some extent, that person's feelings. Natural communicators, particularly salespeople, seem to adopt this flexible style very easily, and mirroring has become one of their successful techniques. However, like any skill, initially it may have to be done consciously, and sometimes it will seem very difficult or contrived. Start mirroring in all sorts of interpersonal situations and notice the improvements in rapport by using this simplest of techniques.

Pacing and leading

The mirroring idea can be taken a step further. It has also been found that the physiology of one person can actually influence the physiology of another. If I consciously *change* my body language, the other person will be inclined to follow my pattern. Therefore, in addition to mirroring to increase rapport with the other party, by 'pacing and leading' you can actually change the state of mind of the person with whom you are communicating. Let us suppose the person is very irate and is speaking quickly in a high-pitched, angry voice. Initially you should mirror his or her method of communicating. To some degree, at least, you will increase your speed of responses and take on their characteristics, so they will appreciate that you have entered into their state of mind. To respond in a slow, cool, very moderated way would probably further inflame the person. Once you have mirrored the individual's style, you can gradually reduce the speed and tone of the conversation, at the same time changing your body posture in such a way that the other person tends to follow. This is done in small stages, waiting until each incremental change in physiology has been mirrored by the other person. In due course, you can sit down or take on a far more relaxed posture, perhaps introducing some humour, and find that you have led the person, through pacing and leading, into a different, more empowering state of mind. Rapport has been maintained throughout, but you have been instrumental in changing a situation for the better. This is a powerful technique for handling a difficult member of a training group or in a meeting. It is much more effective than engaging in arguments with words.

Verbal pacing, however, is also effective, and is something with which we are all familiar. Rather than lead to an argument we often say 'Yes ... but'—agreeing first before going on to give another point of view. In effect we show that we understand 'where the person is at' and how he or she feels, then, once at the individual's *pace*, go on to *lead* where we want him or her to go. Even better is the salesperson's ploy of 'Yes ... *and*'—in which even an objection is turned into an opportunity. So the principle of first pacing, then leading, can apply to any aspect of the communication.

Pacing and leading, as well as simple mirroring, is used by top communicators, even though in many cases they are not aware of their successful process. It is primarily used in one to one situations, but as it can also be applied in smallish groups it has obvious training applications. Once you become familiar with mirroring and feel that you can do it unobtrusively and gain rapport, try pacing and leading.

Congruence   A feature of top communicators is what is termed *congruence*. As perceived by the trainees or students, this means matching what is said with the rest of the communication signs such as body language. When we do not believe strongly in what we are saying, it is usually revealed by the fact that our physiology does not match the words we speak. Even when we try to get this right, those we are communicating with can often tell unconsciously when there is a mismatch. This is akin to the negative chemistry that we sometimes experience on meeting a person for the first time—we don't know why, but somehow we feel that something is wrong. Therefore, before gaining rapport with trainees, the trainer needs to establish this personal congruence. Basically it involves having a clear training outcome, believing in the subject you are communicating, and thereafter 'being yourself'—not consciously intervening in the communication process. Like any other real skill, effective interpersonal communication must eventually become an aspect of our unconscious competence.

We each play many roles in life. For example, during the course of a week, we might be a friend, worker, receiver, giver, parent, teacher, learner, scapegoat, etc. When these varying roles are in agreement, we can be said to be congruent. When they conflict, we are not. Congruence means being together and in agreement, and can apply, not just in relationships with others, but also within oneself. At this level, congruence occurs when all our subpersonalities join together to work for us towards some outcome in a unified way.

A congruent communication is one in which all 'parts' of the person are in agreement. An incongruent communication is one in which there is some disagreement between the parts of a person—a mixed message is received. This can either be conscious—that is, when we are lying—or unconscious, in the form of doubt, uncertainty or, inner conflict. In an incongruent communication, there will always be a mismatch between the words used and some part of the speech tonality or body language displayed. This incongruence varies from person to person and from time to time. As you begin to know someone well, you can usually tell when there is incongruence in what he or she is saying. You learn to 'read' a person, and this includes that person's moods and feelings, all part of the total communication, as well as what he or she says or does not say. This explains why some trainers are not effective, even when they appear to be acting in a professional manner, and seem to be doing everything correctly.

The skill of detecting congruent and incongruent communications is particularly useful in situations where some action depends on the agreement of others. If their agreement is incongruent (saying yes, for instance, while not seeming to have understood the implications or not being very enthusiastic), the chances are they will forget to carry out the action. An incongruent communication does not fully 'register', so the outcome is unlikely to be achieved. Also, as we have already seen, only the communicator can take responsibility for the communication, and his or her outcome. You need the skill to gather information to find out what the considerations and doubts of the other person are, and either the ability to meet these in some way, or, if you cannot, readiness to changing your outcome.

We looked earlier at the importance of an ecology check, and also met the idea that every behaviour follows some positive intention. Incongruence also results when our behaviours seek, unconsciously, to bring about different and conflicting intentions; therefore until we establish exactly what our intentions are, and clarify our personal goals, there is danger of a behaviour or communication being incongruent and thus ineffective.

Meetings

Meetings are an important part of communication in any organizational setting, and NLP makes its own contribution. The principle of a well-formed outcome applies as much in a group or meeting situation as in achieving an individual goal. Here is a basic format that can be applied to any meeting, for any purpose, involving any number of people.

The ABC, etc., of effective meetings

A. Aim for a well-formed outcome. If necessary, re-read the tests in Chapter 3.
B. Balance structure and freedom to optimize well-being and creativity.
C. See, hear, feel, sensory data and stay in uptime. Be aware; be alert.
D. Dovetail desires, and seek mutual outcomes.
E. Entertain flexibility of thought and behaviour throughout. Check Chapter 6 on reframing, which will help when you are faced with apparently irreconcilable objectives.

Be prepared

Here are some more specific rules you can use as a further checklist. For meetings to be effective you need:

- a well-formed outcome (remember the criteria for clear goals);
- evidence criteria (what will be the sensory specific results of the outcome, what will we see, hear and feel?);
- an optimum environment designed to facilitate the outcome;
- some attendance rule—for example, two-thirds, or whatever ratio has been found to work best;
- to establish rapport with each participant;
- to check the resourcefulness of each participant.

The PEGASUS meeting format

All this can be summarized using a simple mnemonic:

P   present outcomes
E   explain evidence procedure
G   gain agreement on outcomes
A   activate sensory acuity
S   summarize each major decision
U   use frames (as if, relevancy [below], and Meta Model [Chapter 11])
S   summarize the next step.

Information-gathering frames

The meaning of a communication is the response it produces. NLP views communication in terms of its effectiveness rather than as a message, behaviour or other input, however efficiently carried out. Better understanding can be obtained by the use of information-gathering frames, of which there are several types. These are further examples of reframing (covered in Chapter 6) but are used particularly in meetings, interviews, or other information-gathering communication situations.

Outcome frame   An outcome frame identifies and clarifies the purpose of any interaction. The outcome identified is a mutual one, and has to meet the criteria for a well-formed outcome (see Chapter 3). You have to know what you will see, hear and/or feel when you have realized your outcome.

'As if' frame   This allows you to explore possibilities and alternatives. For examples: 'If you were me what would you do?' or, 'If you did know the answer, what might it be?'

Consequence frame   This is useful for problem solving and planning, and seeks to identify the consequence of an action. For example: What will happen if we do this? What is the best that can happen? What is the worst that can happen?

Relevancy challenge   This enables you to keep control of any communication, and understand how the other person is thinking. It is used in conjunction with the outcome frame. An example of a relevancy challenge, when the topic of car parking facilities has been raised, might be: 'We're working on the best ways to improve monthly performance, can you explain how car parking facilities will affect this?'

Information-gathering questions and softeners

Questions and communications should be geared towards solutions rather than problems, with an eye always on the desired outcome. Often a solution is buried in generalities, and the skill is to be specific and move the communication on from these generalities to a more sensory-based issue. The least helpful kind of question starts with 'Why', as this often brings up the past with excuses, justifications and rationalizations, taking you away from real life experience, towards concepts and beliefs. Instead, ask 'where?', 'when?', 'who?', 'what?' and 'how?', to gain more specific and useful information about real life. However, such questions can often sound confronting to the hearer, so become skilled in using 'softeners' that allow you to probe sensitive areas and make incisive questions quite gently. For example: 'I'm wondering if you can ...' or, 'I'm curious to know if ...' or 'What I'm asking myself is ...' and so on. Always respect the other person when gathering information. Stay in sensory awareness and be flexible to achieve your mutual outcomes. Always remember that each of you is seeing things through your own unique, perceptual map and none of you has experienced true reality.

Training applications

The principles and techniques of effective communication in NLP have widespread applications in training and development. Any professional trainer knows that once strong rapport has been established with a group of trainees, a successful activity or programme is likely to follow. Basic rapport seems to be a far bigger factor than either the technical aspects of the communication, or even the content of the training itself. We know, for example, that where training 'scores' very high on presentation and low on technical content, the net learning is still greater than where content is excellent, but presentation is weak. It seems to depend on the process rather than the content of communication. And even the most sophisticated communication is rendered useless if it is not delivered with congruence.

Increasingly the trainer's role is one of facilitator and coach, and the days of 'chalk and talk' seem to be numbered (although there is the danger that high-tech equivalents of chalk replace the old version of one-sided communication). In this new situation, the principles and techniques of NLP assume a new importance.

Everything we have learned from NLP, besides helping the professional trainer, is of course, potential material for course contents. Some of the most popular training programmes, such as negotiation skills, presentation skills, appraisals, interviews and so on, involve—or should involve—all the principles and techniques that we have covered. Thus the design of these programmes can be made more effective by introducing the up-to-date 'communication technology' of NLP. The pacing and leading technique, for example, is most powerful when used in a negotiation situation, giving us enormous power to bring about our own outcomes. It can also be used when handling staff individually, either in a disciplinary situation or where particular sensitivity is needed. We now have technology to achieve the vital rapport upon which successful mutual outcomes depend. All of this applies just as well to chairing and taking part in meetings, so with a little imagination you can improve both your personal communication skills as a trainer, and the design and content of training programmes.

6 Reframing

Most communication problems result from an inability to understand what the other person wants and how he or she behaves or feels. Because he or she has a different understanding of a situation, the message of the communication is received in a different way to what was intended. We have already met the presupposition that the success of a communication is measured on the basis of whether or not it produces its desired outcome. When we do not get the results we want, assuming we have made a genuine attempt to express our message, it is likely that we have failed to understand how the other party perceives something—how he or she thinks. We tend to concentrate on the message or the medium rather than the person to whom we are addressing the communication. The NLP presupposition that 'the map is not the territory' says it all; we are trying to communicate using different maps, so it is not surprising that we make little progress. As we saw, the best communication happens when there is rapport, and rapport happens when we understand each other's maps of reality. We often talk about putting ourselves in the other person's shoes, or seeing things from the other person's point of view, or getting on the same wavelength. Getting the other perspective on a matter, or several perspectives, helps understanding and communication.

The term used is *reframing*. It involves a transformation of meaning; by putting a situation into a different frame of reference, we can gain insights and understanding that we would otherwise have missed. A neutral or negative behaviour, event or situation can be transformed into a positive one, often creating benefits and opportunities, and more choices for achieving outcomes. A 9-year-old boy takes a run at a 40-year-old man and head-butts him in the stomach. This would seem to be quite unacceptable behaviour. But if they are father and son playing in the park the meaning is changed—the activity is reframed. Seeing things in a different light, another party will react and behave differently. If the boy has recently recovered from a major accident and is rapidly getting back to his old pugnacious self, a further angle on the scene—another frame—is revealed. And each reframe helps towards better understanding. In each case we get a better idea of someone else's map. Now picture the same occurrence in the foyer of the boy's school on the evening of a parent–teacher consultation. Change the frame slightly to make the topic of the parent–teacher interview immediately preceding the head-butting incident some shining school results that leave the child with all but wings. That puts a different light on things, perhaps. Then make the parent–teacher consultation the final warning before the boy's suspension. Each new perspective will reframe the situation, giving it new meaning and new significance.

Often we do not know the real meaning behind a behaviour. Although you can literally get into someone else's shoes, you cannot get into a person's mind. But there is nevertheless enormous benefit in being able to reframe a situation, and see things from as many viewpoints as possible. Even the *possibility* of a different meaning is usually enough to change your attitude and behaviour. In some cases, having reframed a situation, you will say or do nothing, being calm and rational when you might otherwise have been completely enraged. If you are communicating, you have a better chance of achieving your outcome if you have more perspectives on a situation.

Perceptual positions

These perspectives are just the points of view from which we perceive the world at any time. But there are basic differences in the point of view we are taking, and these are points of view known as *perceptual positions*. The first position is your own personal point of view. The second position is the other person's in any interaction. The third perceptual position—or fourth, fifth and so on—is the point of view of a third party or outside observer. This is also known as the meta position.

In order to gain understanding of an event or communication, we need to be able to see things from as many points of view as possible. Therefore, we need to see as the other person sees, get into his or her shoes, or whatever metaphor is suitable. The skill lies in recognizing different perspectives rather than reconciling them. By getting more perspectives you will be getting a glimpse into other perceptual maps as valid as your own, and at the same time your own map of reality will become richer. You will also start to see more choices, and better ways to achieve your outcomes. You will have more control over how you feel and your attitude to people and issues. A wise person is one who can occupy many perceptual positions. Just by thinking of a problem or issue in terms of perceptual positions—without applying any of the techniques described later—you will be able to reframe it.

Logical levels

Learning and change happen at different levels, and NLP has a model of logical levels to illustrate this. This simple model also offers another way to get different perspectives on behaviour.

- **Environment**   This is our surroundings, and the things and people around that we react to.
- **Behaviour**   This is what we do, our actual behaviour, regardless of what we are capable of doing.
- **Capability**   This level comprises the skills and strategies we use in life; they are groups of behaviour that we have learned, and they are available to us in specific circumstances.
- **Beliefs**   At this level we behave in accordance with what we think is true, including about ourselves. A belief can either empower us to successful action or act in a limiting way. All our actions are based on some supporting belief.
- **Spiritual**   At a higher level we operate on the basis of who we are, our core values and our purposes—i.e. our identity.

As a trainer, for example, you might behave on one or more of these levels. At the lowest environment level you may react to the physical venue, a spare meeting room, for instance, for an informal group discussion, as compared to a large auditorium in a swish hotel. Struggling through a morning session after a night of sickness, and all the specific behaviour associated, can be seen from the level of actual behaviour. But that does not tell the full story—you are a skilled presenter, especially good at thinking on your feet and gaining rapport with small groups. From the level of your capability, training, and the groups of behaviour and strategies that you usually call upon, a different picture might emerge. But even regardless of your capability, you may believe that some of the group resent being on the course, or that the review will be used for a decision about further training, or that you are better at one-to-one counselling than up-front training. Any such belief is likely to affect your behaviour, but at a different level. Finally, you may not see yourself in this role, or what you are doing may conflict with your core values. Even though you achieve an acceptable technical performance, you are not true to yourself and in the longer term this shows.

These perspectives are important, and can change how we feel about a situation or behaviour. Whatever you *do* may not reflect your capability, your beliefs and values—it may not even reflect what you *are*, let alone allow for the specific environment or circumstances. We can therefore feel very differently about how we or others behave by seeing things at different logical or neurological levels. Sometimes conflict is created, as what you are well capable of, for example, may not reflect your beliefs and identity. You are presented with choices, and you may have to sort out your outcomes.

Timelines

Having considered perceptual positions and logical levels, there is another dimension that also affects how we frame things—time. Some people seem to live in the future, always talking about what they are going to accomplish. Others live in the past, and it seems as though the memories they have are as real as present experience, and more important to them than what the future might hold. Others are able to live in the present, enjoying all the simple pleasures of life without either regrets about the past or worries about the future.

The way we perceive time is another example of how we structure thought differently when building up our individual maps of reality. If events are likely to be changed or overtaken by time, they are less likely to affect us emotionally. The simple thought that there will be a 'next time'—another speech to make, another training event, another month's figures—can take the heat out of the most traumatic situation. And when feelings are under control, we are likely to have more choices about how we perceive something and what we do about it.

Thought structures as affecting time, or 'timelines', are coded in the same way as other thoughts, and can be described as representations, with different submodalities. Some people, for example, 'see' the future as big and bright when they imagine it, and the past as less vivid. Or the reverse may be the case, which quickly begins to explain how different people are attracted to either the past or the future. Some people see a series of still rather than movie pictures. The phrase 'the future looks bright' can be a literal description for some people, as can 'putting the past behind you', which is where some people's thoughts about the past seem to be located. By identifying the modalities and submodalities of memories and future events, you will be able to learn how you structure time mentally. Then by switching submodalities— perhaps changing the location of an image, or its size and intensity— you will change your perception of time. A future event can thus be made more attractive, and so become a more compelling inner goal. A desempowering memory can be reduced to the level at which it loses its power.

Time reframing is a valuable control tool. Imagine, for instance, you have a distasteful event to face in the coming weeks. Imagine it was yesterday, and is now over, with whatever consequences—including the worst possible scenario. Or imagine it happened five years ago, and is now just a dim, insignificant memory. How might that change how you feel about the upcoming event or activity? You can start to have personal control and create choices.

Examples of reframing

There are examples of reframing all around us. An article you buy is very expensive until you compare it with other things on which you spend money. What might it cost you (in the longer run, perhaps) if you did *not* buy the article? Or how do you value the pleasure it will bring you? What about reframing in a family situation? From time to time we measure the performance of a child, academically, socially or in a sport, for instance. But our worlds are so small (that is our perceptual maps are so limited) that we often fail to put things into even a reasonable frame. What are we comparing with? An older brother or sister? The rest of the class at school? Or yourself and your own brothers and sisters? Or the village genius? Even a casual consideration of the frame of reference can dramatically change both how we feel and what we do. By thinking in this way we give ourselves choices, opening up new ways to act, and new ways to achieve our own outcomes. Reframing never constrains us. You and I are free to compare our children with the best in the land or the county borstal. The wider our perspective and the more we can get things into context, the richer will be our understanding, and the more effective our behaviour.

Context and content reframes

NLP usually divides reframes into context reframes and content reframes. When you reframe the context you in effect ask 'In what situations would this behaviour be viewed differently?' Some unsociable habits are acceptable in other foreign cultures. What is acceptable in one work situation is frowned upon in another. In the case of the child at school you can imagine the different context of the park.

When you reframe the content of behaviour or an incident, you focus on whatever you want to, and give it whatever meaning you wish. By changing the boy, the man, the relationship, or the circumstance, you change the possible meaning. The same happens when considering the 'expensive' article. Thus, a content reframe *focuses* on any aspect of a situation to get other possible meanings, and a context reframe takes a *wide-angle view* of the whole situation. You reframe by asking the questions: What else could this mean? What is the positive value of this behaviour? How else can I describe what is happening? What aspects of the situation might have a different meaning? The expensive article, for instance, might have been viewed differently if it was the person's fiftieth birthday or if he or she had just learned of a terminal illness. The distinction between content and context reframing is not important other than in helping us to gain more perspectives. The significant thing is not to view things through blinkered eyes, or with limited perceptual maps.

A new look at training

Reframing can be applied to any behaviour including any aspect of training and development. By considering the principle at work you will become more instinctively aware not only of reframes, but also of the practical uses to which you can apply the principles. Let me risk some examples which I hope will not limit your own creativity, which is what reframing is all about. First, the cost of training. Most companies produce frightening figures about the cost of winning a new customer, as compared, for example, with the minimal financial cost of servicing an existing one with basic customer service. Front-line employees usually have less training than their functional and managerial colleagues, yet often hold enormous power when it comes to influencing customers, existing or potential. The cost of training when seen in the context of losing a customer—and having to win another one—or even losing a specific sale, can turn training into a money-spinning or money-saving investment. Similarly, in the context of the person's salary, or of what a competing company spends, or of the last three years' departmental training expenditure, a different 'story' might emerge. In fact reframing can be used to reveal a T&D spend as being pathetically low or ridiculously high. It can make training look good or bad.

Advertisers are using reframes constantly to bring about their various objectives. But whether you are an advertiser or consumer, a trainer or delegate, or a CEO or receptionist, reframing gives you a better understanding, and more choices. Also, as we saw in one of the presuppositions, three or more choices is what you should be aiming for if you want the freedom to bring about your own outcomes. But you are then responsible for what you do with your understanding and how you use your choices. NLP is concerned with creating new frames, rather than how the new 'truths' or insights are used.

As a further training example, imagine a delegate in a seminar who has had his eyes closed for the last 15 minutes or so. This can be disconcerting for the most seasoned professional trainer. What does reframing do? A context reframe will consider the circumstances in which such behaviour would be acceptable or laudable. In a large conference perhaps? In church? In a foreign country or different culture? Meanings can then be postulated about the actual situation. Perhaps the delegate has had a sleepless night with his new baby. He may be suffering from a migraine headache and cannot bear the light. He may find a mannerism of the presenter unbearable and gets more out of the seminar with his eyes closed. He may be practising some visualization that was the subject of an earlier training course. He may be fascinated by what is being said and is able to concentrate more fully with his eyes closed. Any such reframe is certain to take some emotion out of the situation for the trainer (where, for the moment, the problem seems to lie). Even the law of averages would reduce the chances, in the presenter's mind, of some career-shattering situation. In this actual situation the presenter, after a humbled professional pride and rising blood pressure, made a jocular remark about what the delegate had been doing the previous night, only to learn that the last explanation was the case—the delegate was concentrating intensely in a way that worked best for him. Not surprisingly, the presenter then lost the attention and respect of his best disciple. The other delegates were familiar with this person's idiosyncrasy even in day-to-day conversations. A few moments of reframing thought was all that was needed. The preferred behaviour of the presenter is hardly worth discussing—we could all suggest ideas—and his behaviour could hardly have been as ineffective as it was. The simplest of reframes would have sufficed. Other viewpoints are bound to produce a wider range of possible behaviour—and results. It pays to create options by seeing things in a different light. Even if you do nothing, you cannot avoid changing your feelings and attitude as new frames are perceived.

Having established the principle, specific techniques can help in reframing. These can be used by the trainer in addressing any aspects of T&D and can also be incorporated into the content of programmes concerned with idea generation, problem solving or communication.

Sleight of Mouth

Let us begin with a technique called Sleight of Mouth, the term alluding to the magician's sleight of hand. This stimulates other perspectives on any problem using a simple model. I have used a 'problem-statement' from the field of T&D as an illustration, but you can use the technique on any specific problem you face.

The value of training, it seems, cannot be measured to the satisfaction of all the parties involved, including those responsible for funding decisions. Before applying the technique the problem is clearly worded as a problem-statement, and it is worth doing this carefully. 'The value of training cannot easily be measured' should suffice for our present example, although in practice it might apply to a specific programme or course. As Figure 6.1 shows, responses, in the form of statements or questions, are then suggested from different angles—such as a positive or negative viewpoint, a general or more focused view, an abstract or more personal perspective, and so on. Starting at the top, the *Model of the world* lifts the problem to a very general or cosmic level—producing a more philosophical perspective. Such a response, for example, might be 'Value is a very personal thing' or 'It's difficult to measure qualities rather than quantities' or even 'Life is full of such uncertainties'. The next perspective, going clockwise, *Apply to self*, attempts to personalize a problem or issue —to put the spotlight on the problem-owner rather than the problem. So you might respond 'That's an interesting personal point of view' or 'How have you (try to incorporate *'you'*) come to that particular conclusion?' Carry on round, making up responses—several if you wish—from each of the different perspectives.

There are a few important things to remember when using this and some other reframing techniques. First, you are not producing *answers* at this stage, although something might well occur to you as responses are formulated. If answers could be produced from a technique in such a pat way, the problem would not really qualify as a problem in the first place. Rather, you are attempting to get other perspectives. One of these might well produce the 'aha' which leads to either a better

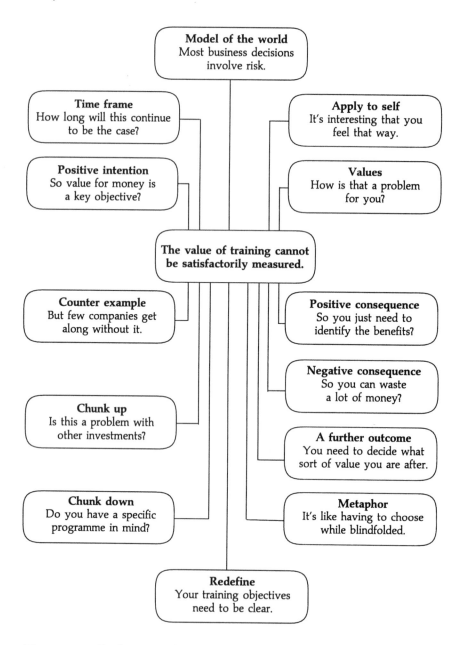

Figure 6.1 *Sleight of Mouth*

definition of the problem, another question or a solution. Like brainstorming, the purpose is to generate as many ideas as possible. If a brainwave does emerge, keep going—you may get more, then you have more choices.

Second, the more responses you can create from each perspective, the greater the chance of cracking open a problem or issue. Therefore, be prepared to go round the model a few times, generating new responses each time. For instance, there is no limit to the number of metaphors that might offer an association with the problem. What might seem naïve to you might 'click' with someone else who has a different personal map of experience and will thus make different associations.

Third, do not worry if you cannot think of responses from a particular viewpoint. This is not an exhaustive technique for the left brain with fixed rules and black and white answers, but a stimulus for the creative right brain. Every situation is different and these are just suggested perspectives that usually help—think of some more if you can. But in most cases you should be able to suggest at least 13 angles on a problem, and usually a great many more. More often than not one or two of these will move things forward. In other cases an idea might come later, unexpectedly, but clearly triggered by addressing the problem in this way.

Finally, you cannot avoid doing some *thinking*—and creative thinking at that. The more creative your responses, the more choices you will produce, and the better will be your eventual solution. The model is a checklist or stimulus for your naturally creative brain.

This technique can apply to literally any problem statement —a specific human relation matter, a departmental of functional issue, something of corporate importance, or a very personal matter. It should be a *genuine* problem, preferably an intractable one, as this is where creative reframing comes into its own. If a spreadsheet or computer program will give the answer, you do not need to resort to your right brain. But most real life problems are not solved in that way—they need to be reframed. You might start by thinking of three pressing issues that you want to tackle. Express them as simple problem-statements—and a little practice at this helps—then work your way round the model.

The Sleight of Mouth model can be used in a group setting, in which case a wider range of responses will be generated. Typically one person will present a problem, and the group will apply their creative skills. The technique is also quite effective on a DIY basis.

Points of View

Another technique is called Points of View. This is particularly useful in interpersonal situations when people hold different points of view. We often use expressions like 'She just doesn't understand' or 'I simply can't get through to him'. In this case we make up sentences using words that force a different point of view:

good, bad, right, wrong, stupid, smart, better, worse.

Using the example 'She doesn't understand' and these words, we can come up with the following sentences:

It's good that she doesn't understand **because** she might not be able to face things.

It's bad that she doesn't understand **because** it's ruining our relationship.

It's right that she doesn't understand **because** she doesn't have all the facts.

It's wrong that she doesn't understand **because** that's what she's paid to do.

It's stupid that she doesn't understand **because** she is coming off worse.

It's smart that she doesn't understand **because** she can't be held responsible.

It's better not to understand **than** do what she does out of malice.

It's worse not to understand **than** not to even listen.

As in the previous technique, you may be able to suggest several 'points of view' using each triggering word. Alternatively, you might struggle to think of any in particular cases, or it might seem stupid and pointless. Again, the model is to stimulate creative thought, and it is your own creativity in devising different points of view that will unlock a problem and change a situation. You can use or discard a technique as you wish. It's the principle—in this case the need for other points of view to help understanding and increase your options—that you need to stick with. With practice, reframing can become an intuitive way of thinking which will be more effective in bringing about your outcomes than analytically based problem-solving techniques.

Reversals

Other techniques have been used in business situations which, while not strictly NLP techniques, help with reframing. In the case of Reversals, you start with a problem-statement just as in the Sleight of Mouth technique, but the statement is then *completely reversed*. For example, 'The value of training cannot easily be measured' would be reversed to state 'The value of training can be easily and accurately measured', or something that similarly reverses the original meaning. Using this new 'truth', you then exercise your creative mind in thinking of issues raised by the new statement, or what might follow from it. For instance:

- Training could be carried out according to rational criteria.
- It could compete with other investments on the basis of the returns it gives.
- There need not be subjectivity in allocating financial and other resources.
- Training could be sold more easily to trainees on the basis of value to them as well as the company.
- Different kinds of training might be subject to standard evaluation.
- Top management could be readily convinced of the effectiveness of particular training.

- 'Do we train?' would not be the question, but rather 'What training is of best value to us?'
- Ineffective training would be discontinued, and resources redirected more effectively.
- Training personnel would have important feedback as to their own effectiveness.
- Training provision might be standardized with corresponding economies of scale on the basis of consistent high returns.
- Scarce funds could be competed for even in difficult economic times on the basis of known returns.
- Training would be seen as an important profit earner alongside mainstream products and services.
- The annual training budget would lose some of its politics.
- There would be a better basis for comparing internal and external training provision.
- Capital investment could be made on a sound economic basis.
- The professional standing of training and development staff would improve.

Issues such as these are thus elicited from a reversal. Each in turn is then considered, to see what further issues, questions or opportunities are suggested by the thoughts triggered. Measurable training might suggest, for instance, that more attention is given to evaluation techniques, where progress is being made presently but on a very piecemeal basis. That is, maybe there is more we can do in the area of evaluation, with all its subjectivity. The benefits identified in the reversal exercise make the extra focus more clearly worth while. In cases where certain training *does* lend itself to accurate evaluation (such as shorter term skills training for selling, debt collection, production processes, quality where it is measurable, etc.) there might be a case for channelling more funds into these areas to allow competition with other financial demands.

'How else might training gain a stronger place corporately?' is a key question that might emerge from a reversal exercise. A board level training appointment? A link to long-term funding (to rank alongside a new canteen, plant, car park or major product development) to avoid the vagaries of recurring annual funding? A consideration of external vs internal provision, even given the problems of evaluation? A profit centre, free to provide externally and subject to outside competition? Other approaches to 'selling' training to top management might follow. Other ways in which training staff can get feedback about effectiveness is another angle that might be developed; or the importance of setting clearer training objectives as a precursor to better evaluation of achievement.

Note that any one of the 'angles' that emerge from the issues raised by reversals, is itself amenable to further reframing using the Sleight of Mouth or other techniques. Simply rephrase the reversal as a new problem-statement, such as 'Stronger board level support for training and development is needed'. Another value of creative rather than analytical techniques is that you often identify and possibly solve other problems, and opportunities are spotted which were never even considered when you first defined your problem. These are always a welcome bonus.

Reframing sets no limits on what is possible. It always increases choices. The reversal technique can be applied to any problem-statement and will often elicit ideas when a more marginal rethink does not work. It is ideal for strategic rethinking in a world of changing markets and technology when original, radical thinking is necessary if you are to remain competitive.

Generating problem-statements

How are the problem-statements generated? You may have no shortage of problems to which to apply your NLP principles, but some comments on problem generation may be useful. One way is to make a list of all the current problems in your department or section, applying reversals to each of them and working through all the issues that emerge. By drawing on other training staff, line and functional managers, and also trainees, you are likely to get not just plenty of volume, but also to reflect the different aspects of the issues. Typically problems keep recurring from different sources and in different guises and these are likely to be the important key issues that need to be reframed.

Most managers and professional trainers are familiar with SWOT techniques, listing strengths, weaknesses, opportunities and threats, which is usually applied to the company, a business unit, or a function or department. This is a useful form of analysis, but is not a very creative tool, often listing 'standard' company factors from training course to training course. True to left-brain processing, it sees parts rather than the whole. It is ideal, however, for initial problem generation, although new problems or issues usually emerge when some creative reframing is brought to bear. Each of the statements is usually amenable to a full reversal 'treatment', so that even minor aspects of the business are opened up to reframing. A single weakness might thus be turned into a strength or even a major opportunity using such techniques. A major threat might turn out to be the next big profit earner.

One of the skills of problem generation is to turn an otherwise positive statement into something that needs creative attention. Few major creative changes happen when things seem to be going well. It is usually when a problem becomes stark, or when we face major upheaval, that the mind excels at producing solutions. Having done a SWOT analysis, the 'problem' with opportunities, for example, is that they have not yet been *realized*—otherwise they would now be embedded in the strengths of the company in the form of products, markets, people and accrued wealth. As a *problem*, you will focus on how to turn the opportunity into a strength or bottom-line reality.

We can also be complacent about strengths. When compared with some competitors (beginning to think holistically), an obvious strength might not be so obvious, and nor will it necessarily remain a strength when everything around is changing, inside and outside the organization. For the Sleight of Mouth problem-statement the skill is to express SWOT statements so that they *need* creativity—they beg some new perspectives. 'We are financially secure' (strength) is unlikely to set the creative juices flowing. 'We are on a cash flow knife edge' (approximate reversal), however, is a challenging problem with the important implicit outcome of survival.

One of the purposes of the reversal technique, in addition to finding new perspectives, is to create the image of a motivating and empowering reality. What seems like a strength is *imagined* as a weakness so that, at least, steps might be identified to ensure that the strength is maintained and built upon. Usually opportunities and threats can be seen as different sides of the same coin. Re-expressing in clear problem terms gives the creative mind its starting point. Reversals keep the 'flip side' in view.

Reframing in the training function

A reframing culture makes for excellent companies, and such creativity can be used profitably in the vital T&D function. For example, with the threat of major training cutbacks a company might consider structuring T&D on a profit centre rather than a cost centre basis, with all the changes in effectiveness and efficiency that that often entails. But those very changes might turn out to be opportunities for better training provision and all the business benefits that will bring. By reframing threatening situations *before* they are realized (and for every training function that was forced into a profit centre operation, many others, and their companies, no longer exist) actions can be taken that take control of a situation.

Usually decisions about the whole training function happen by default rather than design from business circumstances that have no bearing on whether training is a viable long-term investment. There is usually a shortage of profit or cash and any indirect overhead is a target. Training, as much as any other function, has been at the mercy of stop–go policies and the feast and famine of the surrounding business climate. By reframing in the relatively good times, surprises can be minimized. A strength 'We have excellent training buildings and facilities' on reversal would raise important questions, such as 'Why *should* we have buildings?' or 'What if we did *not* have such resources?'

or 'Could we be selling on our facilities?' or 'Are we really using these facilities in the best way?'. Training and development is ripe for new creative thinking—for reframing. But NLP, or reframing for that matter, is not just a set of techniques, however powerful these have been proved to be; it is a whole way of thinking.

Acting with awareness

The creative right brain works largely unconsciously, but there are things we can do consciously to foster greater awareness and see more perspectives. Here are some practical things you can do:

1 Change who you are, pretend to be someone else—anyone else. Try to see things from outside yourself and others.
2 Change what you do—take up some new hobby or activity. Change your focus of attention in your work.
3 Change where you do things. For example, change your lunch venue and meet people in a different location. Perhaps rearrange your office or home furniture until it feels like a different room.
4 Change when you do things. Move regular appointments to different times in the day. Change your sequence of daily routines so that you do things at different times.
5 Change why you do things; try to act in accordance with some reason other than the real one for doing what you are doing. Invent new reasons and behave accordingly. Give yourself some secret agenda; for instance, to make people feel good or happy, or to notice beauty around you in the world. See how your feelings and behaviour change when you change why you do things.
6 Change how you do things. Do some everyday task in a different way.

We have a natural tendency to see things and do things in familiar ways. Most belief system issues arise when we find ourselves in situations of change. Although it starts inside, reframing is all about change. Initiating and managing this process of change involves that person:

● wanting to change
● knowing how to implement the behaviours and skills required for that change
● getting the opportunity to apply them in a context that will actually produce the desired outcome.

The first requirement is often met when considering goals. A desirable outcome often requires change, and the attractiveness of the goal provides the motivation for the change. The second requirement is well fulfilled by the techniques you have learned in this chapter, and other techniques such as mirroring that will produce the rapport you need with others. But even techniques are subject to the underlying need for a clear goal, sensory acuity (and we have just seen ways in which you can act with greater awareness) and flexibility of behaviour. The turning point, and perhaps the key to successful behaviour, is often when we see something in a new light. Reframing is therefore a crucial part of change and achievement.

7 A better state of mind

Most people will agree that what we achieve is determined by what we do; that is, our behaviour. In practice, it is not easy to account for great differences in achievements or results just by observing behaviour. For instance, interpersonal skills involve all manner of body language and nuances of communication, which are not easy to observe let alone to copy to achieve the same results. Differences in feelings, attitudes and beliefs are even more difficult to account for, yet result in very different behaviours and consequent achievement from person to person. If you *feel* particularly good, or efficient, one day, you will probably *behave* in such a way that you fulfil more of your goals or outcomes. If, on the other hand, you do not feel quite on form, then your performance can drop dramatically. In both these cases, you have not changed your fundamental resources, or level of knowledge, or portfolio of skills— you are simply subject to the vagaries of feelings, many of which you perhaps cannot account for. Sometimes these feelings become entrenched as habits of thought and take the form of attitudes. If, for example, you tend to look on the negative side of a situation, this is an attitude that will fundamentally affect all your behaviour and, of course, will severely limit your achievements. If, on the other hand, you set out with an optimistic attitude, or *positive* habits of thought, you will tend to match that with both behaviour and results. These attitudes, and even more transient feelings, represent a massive variable in individual performance and achievement. Control over your state—how you feel—enables you to communicate more effectively and achieve your outcomes.

Thus, our state of mind, or how we feel, affects all our behaviour. How can we change how we feel and thus change our behaviour and our achievements? In Chapter 4 we learned about the language of thinking, including how we inwardly sense by seeing, hearing and feeling, and thus experience reality. We also met the idea of submodalities, or characteristics of our inner seeing, hearing and feeling that give an entirely unique and personal picture of our thought processes as distinct from the content of those thoughts. How we feel about something is tied up with these submodalities. Fortunately, not only can we identify them as we gain practice in using our inner representation systems, but they can be *changed* to affect our behaviour and performance.

Changing how you feel

Let us begin with a memory. Think about an occasion when you achieved something worth while and experienced a happy or 'empowering' state of mind. Relive the experience in as much detail as possible, first through one representation system, then the others. Start with *seeing* everything associated with the memory. In looking at these sights, think about the various submodalities I suggested, rather like the vision control on a television set, and check the characteristics or submodalities that apply to that particular memory recall. Is the picture clear? Is it in full colour or black and white? Is it a large panoramic view, or smaller? Is it framed? Is it life-size or smaller or larger than life? Is the picture blurred? Is it in focus? And, very importantly, do you see what is happening *as if through your own eyes* so that you cannot see yourself, but you can see other people and circumstances around you. Or do you appear in the picture—as if you are looking through the eyes of a third party? Seeing the experience through your own eyes is called 'associated'; recalling the event through the eyes of a third party is termed 'dissociated'. See which applies in the case of a pleasant, success-type memory that you recall. If need be refer back to Chapter 4 where I gave some typical submodalities as a check-list. Identify as many of these characteristics as possible, or others not listed. This exercise will give you clues about your *state of mind* at these times.

Identifying submodalities

Having spent some time on the visual memory, move to the hearing representation system and go through the same process, identifying any characteristics about the sounds that you can hear. This is like adjusting the sound controls on your hi-fi. Again, use the submodalities checklist to remind yourself of the different characteristics of the sounds that you might hear—in particular, any human voices that form part of the memory. Then move on to feelings, what is called the *kinaesthetic* representation system, and once again go through the submodalities checklist to see which of these applies.

Having done this, bring together all the sights, sounds and feelings to re-run the experience, in as realistic a way as possible, like a video recording. Then, just for a moment, record your total feelings on having recalled the memory—noting any sensation in your body. Are you more relaxed? Is there any change in your posture, breathing, and so on? Make a note of all of this, then, having come out of the memory experience, notice what state of mind you are now in.

Making use of memories

Usually when we recall an experience in this way we *recreate* not just the visual and hearing memories, but also our state of mind at that time. We feel today just as we felt on that occasion; and this applies however long ago the event occurred. And this is a real, physiological change. If you were to have your blood pressure, breathing rate and other physical body indicators checked before your memory experience and after, you would probably show an *actual* change. Body and mind are linked, and any change in one affects the other. You have changed the way you feel simply by an act of memory—in fact by *thinking*. In this case, because you recalled a happy experience, you feel happier. A simple, conscious process of thought has altered your state of mind, and will inevitably affect your behaviour and achievements.

To check this out further, think of an *unpleasant* memory—one where the event is painful, distasteful or embarrassing—and go through the same process of identifying each representation system and its submodalities. After a little practice it becomes quite possible, even going back many years. Recalling a bad memory will not be very pleasant, but be assured that the benefits from doing this could far outweigh the pain of the brief recall. Then, having done this exercise, check now how you feel. You will probably find that the painful *state* has been recalled along with the individual memories. But you will probably also find that the submodalities or characteristics of what you experienced were different to those of the happy memory. Once again, as with a more pleasant memory, you have actually *changed your state* to what it was in that early activity or experience.

From this exercise you can see that it is quite possible to change how you feel, regardless of whether the feelings are pleasant or painful. You can do this whenever you wish, choosing states you have known in the past that might empower you in the present. This process will take some practice, even in the case of happy memories. Not everyone can easily recall the three main representation systems, let alone the detailed characteristics of the memory recordings.

Turning behaviour into empowering feelings

Before considering how you can use the above techniques to change your behaviour and thus bring about better results, let us consider an even simpler way to change our state of mind. We saw earlier that our behaviour is closely related to how we feel. But it also works in reverse: how we feel is very closely related to how we behave. It is rather like the old conundrum: Do I whistle because I'm happy, or am I happy because I whistle? If you observe people in a happy state of mind, noticing what they are doing with their *bodies*—their physiology—you will have an idea of the kind of behaviour that is linked to a happy state of mind. Or watch someone who is very depressed and unhappy, and you will see the kind of behaviour that is linked to an unhappy or disempowering state of mind. The physical characteristics are fairly standard. If you assume the *behaviour* of a particular state, you will tend to induce that state. If you assume a slouched posture with a frown and a slow shuffling walk—the demeanour of a depressed, sad, painful person, for example—you will actually *adopt* that state of mind. Your whole physiology signals the state to your brain. If, on the other hand, you act the part of happiness, success and confidence, then in a strange way your mind will follow what your body is doing. Therefore, to bring about a desired state here are two powerful approaches: first, *think* appropriate thoughts; and, second, *act* in an appropriate way. Both are within *your* control. *You* are the master.

How can you use this ability to change how you feel in everyday personal and work situations? Start with a particular activity or forthcoming event—perhaps one that is already scheduled in your diary—that you would like to feel confident about as that would increase your chances of success. Otherwise create an imaginary situation that could actually occur in the coming weeks or months—an event that you know you would feel anxious about, or would cause a state of mind that is *disempowering.* Choose an activity that you singularly dislike (maybe because of the people associated with it) and which causes some mental pain.

Future pacing   Now go through the process of *future pacing* or mental rehearsal (the term more widely used outside NLP). This is the reverse of remembering; this time you project forward, but use the same representation systems (seeing, hearing and feeling) in respect of the event or activity you want to improve. Go through each submodality in detail, just as you did with the memories, and make a note of what you experience. You will then finish off with a profile, or mind-picture, of two different activities—a happy one from your memory and the less pleasant one you imagine. Each will probably have a different profile of submodalities or characteristics. For present purposes, the fact that the *content* of these is different is of no consequence—one image might involve taking part in a sport at the weekend, and the other running a meeting at work. The important thing is the *characteristics* of the thoughts. Compare the two experiences and note any *differences.*

You will probably find that the submodalities do differ as between your memory and the mental rehearsal of the future event, just as they do between a 'good' and a 'bad' memory. It is these *differences* in the characteristics of the thought processes—the different variety of submodalities—that account for what we call our state of mind; in other words, how we feel. If you feel good about something, you cannot explain this just by the content of the memory or imagination. There is no logical reason, for instance, why one person gets into a state of fear about something which causes another person delight. But there *is* a distinction in the way we process those thoughts—in the modalities (representation systems) and submodalities that make up our unique mental experience. Thus, having isolated these differences, you now know why you feel good on one occasion and bad on another: it is because you see, hear and feel things in a different way. The big questions are: Can we do anything about this? Can we change those thought characteristics? The answer to both questions is Yes, and let us give it a try.

Switching empowering thought patterns

Re-live the future event that you mentally rehearsed, but now *substitute* the submodalities from your happy, confident memory, to replace the submodalities in your future pacing. For instance, if in the happy memory the pictures are large and bright, life-size, panoramic and in full colour, then one by one, change the characteristics of your future activity to match these images. This might seem impossible, but in fact is perfectly possible. You can do almost anything if you *put your mind to it* (quite literally); but do it one step at a time. You can make a picture large or small, you can switch it from black and white to colour and, very importantly, you can change a dissociated picture into an associated one—that is, you can see things as if through your own eyes. Association or dissociation is an important characteristic of how you represent something. So, for instance, if in your mental rehearsal of the forthcoming activity you can see yourself in the picture as if it were being viewed by an outsider, but in your happy memory you were seeing through your own eyes, then switch the future mental picture to become an associated one—get inside the activity and see yourself *through your own eyes.* You now know that an associated picture *to you* is linked with an empowering, confident, happy memory, so you have learned one of the secrets of controlling your state of mind.

Having switched, one by one, all the submodalities you identified in the seeing, hearing and feeling representations systems, note how you feel when you now think about the future activity. You will probably find that you can produce the same state of mind that you felt when you thought about your past happy memory, because your 'state of mind' is simply the combination of these thought characteristics. It is the way that we *process* thoughts, rather than the subject content of the thoughts themselves, that determines how we feel. You have now learned to change how you feel about any future event, and your attitude towards it.

You may want to check this out a bit further. Think of other memories, both bad or good, personal or business, sports or hobbies. You can retrace thoughts back to your childhood. Re-live those memories, identify their characteristics, and watch for any common pattern of thought characteristics as between pleasant and unpleasant, empowering and disempowering ones. When you have found the pattern that is unique to you, you will know the disempowering submodalities you want to replace—and the empowering submodalities you want to replace them with—those you can relate to more successful behaviour and outcomes.

Not only can you change the effect a memory has on you, but you can also change your state of mind with regard to any current or future activity in which you might be involved. The more you practise visualizing mentally, the more skilful you will be at both recognizing and changing these submodalities. This is a very useful skill to develop. Let me repeat that the term visualizing is generally used to include all inner representations, not just visual ones, and you can change any of these. For example, you may wish to concentrate on sounds and feelings.

This is a trainable mental skill. It addresses one of the biggest factors in skill learning—the state of mind we bring to the learning situation, our expectancy of an outcome, and self-image in the field of endeavour.

Speaking to yourself

Most people are familiar with what we call inner dialogue or 'speaking to yourself'—that inner voice which sometimes criticizes, sometimes praises, but always seems to interfere with what we do and think about. The voice may seem to be austere and frightening on occasions, but on recalling a memory or a situation where such a voice is heard, you can deliberately *change* the voice, making it a different tone, a higher or lower pitch, or quicker or slower. If you wish, you can change a man's voice into a woman's, or make it sound like Mickey Mouse. Therefore, without even changing the dialogue, you can easily affect the way you feel by altering these auditory characteristics. Old associations will be lost, and you will gain control over irrational feelings. Voice tonality and volume are, of course, some of the auditory submodalities you have already met, and you can change these just as you changed the brightness or focus of a visual image.

If you are not familiar with the idea of inner dialogue, you can no doubt recollect a memory that involves an actual human voice—maybe the thundering voice of a school teacher, or a boss—and you can make the same changes to those actual memory recordings. Try changing a fearful voice into that of a little child, and notice the different effect. This is another way to control how you feel.

Mental practice

Visualization, or mental rehearsal, has a wide application to all kinds of skills training. The concept has been known for many years, particularly in areas such as sports. Duncan Goodhew, the Olympic gold medallist in swimming, would lie down before a swim and visualize the whole of the event, feeling the water on his body, hearing the sounds of the crowds, and eventually feeling the touch of the tiles that showed that he had won the race. Keeping this state of mental concentration, he would then move to the starting block and proceed into the race, allowing his whole body and muscular system to 'replay' the mental imagery that he had implanted so strongly in his mind. Golfers are also familiar with this technique. Frequently a golfer will visualize a swing, and then entrust what he or she might term 'muscle memory' to carry out the swing. Ben Hogan would not just visualize the golf swing, but the whole trajectory of the ball, how it would land, where it would bounce and where it would stop. He then similarly proceeded to put into operation what he had already clearly imprinted on his mind. Top golfers describe different visualizing 'systems' that work for them.

As well as being supported by a wealth of anecdotal experience, there has been no shortage of research in this area. In one study among high school students the activity concerned free throws in basketball. The measurement was simple, either you scored by dropping the ball into the basket, or you missed. The study involved three groups of basketball players who were at a similar level of competence. The three groups practised for a certain period in three different ways. The first group practised physically for an agreed period each day for the period of the study, then at the end their improvement in average score was computed. The second group similarly practised, not physically, but mentally. For the same period each day they *visualized*, or clearly imagined themselves throwing the ball into the basket. They, too, were measured at the end of the period. The third group was for control purposes only, and they carried out no practice, either physical or mental, during the period of the research. The results were remarkable. The group of students who practised physically showed an average improvement in their hit-rate score of 24 per cent. The group that carried out no form of practice, not surprisingly, had a zero change in their level of competence. But the group that had practised only mentally, not touching a basketball during the whole period of the study, actually improved their average score by 23 per cent—almost to the same level as the group that had 'real' practice every day. Other research has produced equally remarkable results with throwing darts, and in other sports that are easily measurable.

There is one principle involved in this technique of mental rehearsal that makes it so powerful: at one level the mind *cannot tell the difference* between a clearly visualized experience and what we might call reality. In other words, as far as the mind was concerned, the student really *was* shooting basketballs or throwing a dart.

Practising success rather than failure

The significance of these visualization techniques goes even further. Mental 'practice', as well as recording actual images on the brain, deals in successes rather than failure. And what makes the technique so powerful is that we do not practise *misses*. In real life—whether in sports, business, or any other area—for each time you score a hit, you are likely to miss at least once. We have therefore to live with negative memories in the brain, and these memories, which we seem unable to erase, tend to hamper our performance. Technically, if you can throw a dart into a bullseye once, you are physically and mentally able to do it again and again. But this does not happen, and clearly is related to the way we think and feel, and to the negative effect of, perhaps, thousands of 'failure recordings' on the brain. In mental rehearsal we *do not miss*, so every minute's practice is so much more valuable because we are recording, on the very landscape of the brain, successes rather than failures.

One question is frequently asked: 'How, without physical practice, do the sports people remain sufficiently fit to play the sport?' Clearly the way to excellence involves a *combination* of *physical practice* to maintain the peak physical fitness required, and *mental practice* to produce the sheer volume of success recordings which, in turn, gives the level of confidence so vital in any competitive event. The fact that results could be obtained despite the lack of physical practice makes the effect of the mental practice so much more remarkable, counteracting even the loss of physical conditioning. Physical fitness, of course, can be achieved in ways other than actual free throws—or other forms of scoring in other sports. But it is in 'scoring' that failures as well as successes are recorded in the memory, so the most appropriate form of practice, whether for physical conditioning or specific skill, can be chosen. In any event, it seems that the higher the level we want to attain, the more are mental, rather than just physical, factors at play. In many work and personal situations physical fitness is not a major factor, and thus major behavioural changes can be achieved just by mental rehearsal techniques.

Preparing for an interview

The process can be used in any situation in which we need mental confidence: for example, an event, activity or experience that we perhaps are anxious about. It works particularly well in an interview situation. In this case you visualize the interview beforehand in every detail possible, and although it is preferable to have access to the actual room where the interview will take place, so that the imagery is realistic, this is not essential. The power of the technique is not in being able to predict the exact events or circumstances, such as the series of questions in a particular interview; rather, by recording success images on the brain, the level of *confidence* that one needs to do well in such a situation is achieved. People who use this technique readily admit that the questions visualized in advance, and indeed any other detailed circumstances, rarely happen (just like the exam questions you swot for), but they succeed nevertheless in activity after activity because of their induced state of mind. It is the confident state of mind that sees us through stressful situations successfully.

Creating inner confidence

In a T&D situation, the technique can be applied to any public presentation, however small the group, where added confidence is needed. But this is more than 'mind over matter'. Mentally rehearsing skills (say, for a presentation or speech, handling overhead projector and other aids, quoting anecdotes, or whatever) will *actually* improve those skills, just as in the case of basketball or golf. Your added confidence is therefore based on *real* practice (real to the brain, that is) and the consequence is a real improvement in skill.

A particular application of mental rehearsal is where you do not get the necessary degree of opportunity to practise the activity concerned. Perhaps, to stay with the earlier example, you wish to be confident in giving a forthcoming speech to a large group, but as this is not for you an everyday occurrence you do not have a ready audience on which to practise. In this case mental rehearsal is a feasible alternative, and serves the same purpose. Similarly, in various human resources situations, such as difficult interpersonal meetings involving disciplining or even firing, mental rehearsal can be invaluable. Again you may not have the opportunity to build up much experience in making staff redundant, or in some of the less common aspects of interpersonal relationship. By mentally visualizing these occasions as many times as you wish (the mental technique can be carried out very quickly), you will build up the same level of competence and confidence that is shown by any experienced human resources professional, despite your lack of 'real' experience. You can create experience.

Mental rehearsal is a natural experience for all of us, as we know from anticipating a holiday or worrying about something. Used positively, it is a powerful way to change how you feel, and thus your behaviour. It enables you to take more control, creating specific and relevant experience to help you achieve your outcomes.

The technique is also particularly powerful when you are tackling an area of your life in which you have a low self-image. Repeated visualization of successfully performing in a situation that instinctively makes you feel nervous actually builds up your self-image. In the most technical sense, you *become* your new 'self-image' in that particular field or area of activity. Therefore, in addition to being able to change how you feel, as we have seen, you can also change your attitudes and beliefs, specifically what you believe about yourself—what is usually termed your self-image.

Anchoring

In each of these situations I have used the idea of mental rehearsal or visualization to prepare for a future activity, event or situation. Sometimes you can plan several weeks ahead and thus make excellent mental preparation for what you have to face. However, there are occasions when you suddenly find yourself in a situation where you feel particularly vulnerable, or would wish to have greater confidence. The NLP anchoring technique can be used to more or less instantly recall a state of mind that will empower you to do better in a given situation.

You have already learned how you can experience an empowering memory and, through this, bring about a more empowering state of mind. If you can recall such an empowering state of mind at will, you will have a very powerful technique to help in any situation that faces you, even when you have had no notice of the situation. You do this by *anchoring* the state of mind associated with the empowering experience that you wish to recall.

You can use the following method to anchor an empowering state of mind. Concentrate on the procedure you have already learned: recall an empowering experience and choose the state of mind you would like to call on quickly at some future time. Re-live the experience, going through the sights, sounds and feelings as you have already done, and bringing the experience to a climax when you feel your overall state of mind changing into the empowering one that you had at the actual time of the memory. Then 'anchor' this state of mind, by using a simple physiological device. The idea of crossing your fingers is a common one with which we are all familiar, but on this occasion I suggest that you do not cross your fingers as that might have other connotations, and for this purpose you need a *specific* physical anchor that will associate with the specific state of mind you are recalling. Think, therefore, of some other physical anchor. You can crunch up the toes of your left foot, or make a circle with your thumb and middle finger on one hand, or the other—whatever you like. The important thing about an anchor is, first, that it is *unique* to the state that you want to recall, so that whenever you use the anchor it will immediately associate with a particular memory and state of mind; and, second, your anchor should be *discreet*, so that wherever and whenever you need to call upon it, you will feel free to do so without attracting attention or causing embarrassment.

Now do the memory exercise all over again, and again apply your physical anchor. Try to time this so that at the exact time that you use the physical anchor you are experiencing the state that you would like to recall. This will establish a strong link between the anchor and the state being recalled. You can test this. After some 10 or 15 minutes of thinking about something quite different, apply the physical anchor, and notice the change in your state of mind. You should experience not just the memories you recalled earlier, but, more particularly, the state of mind that was associated with your pleasant, positive memory.

Instant empowerment You now have a mechanism you can use to induce a desired state of mind instantly. It can be used in all sorts of day-to-day situations when you would otherwise have felt disempowered or inadequate. For example, assume that you are summoned to a meeting with your boss, or called into a meeting that you have misgivings about, or are facing a particular training group that makes you anxious. As you feel the disempowering state coming on, apply the anchor and notice the positive change in state that will allow you to face the activity more confidently, more positively and more successfully.

It might be that such difficult or distasteful situations are a regular part of your life, in which case you will probably be well aware of what triggers the negative state of mind. It could be the voice of a boss, for example, or walking through a particular door into a particular room. It could be a particular time of day, or day in the week, when a certain activity is about to occur, or it could be something as simple as recognizing the sender's name on an envelope falling on the doormat. If you can become familiar with what triggers a negative state of mind, then not only do you have a physical anchor that can recall a positive state of mind, but you also know exactly when to use it, for maximum effect, to enable you to *pre-empt* the disempowering state of mind.

So far you have just used a physical, or kinaesthetic anchor. But an auditory anchor—perhaps some motivating words—can be added, and this will strengthen the effect. Similarly, a visual image, perhaps drawn from the empowering memory, or some other image you find motivating, can also be associated with any state of mind. All three types of anchor—auditory, visual and physical—can be used, whether in quick succession or simultaneously, to strengthen the association and thus the recall. You will probably find that one anchor has a stronger effect than another (reflecting your sensory preference), and that you can change the effect by the *order* in which you apply the anchors. Adopt whichever system gives the best results.

Anchoring is a very useful and universal mechanism that you can apply when you wish to associate a state of mind with a particular activity or occurrence. However many times you may have failed in the past, you should have a rich database of 'success' memories upon which to draw. Because these success memories are vividly embedded somewhere in your memory, with perseverance and some practice they can be clearly recalled and visualized, and used for future benefit. They are mental assets that can bring you big returns. Use a different anchor for each state of mind you might want to recall. You can *choose* your state of mind. The criterion is whether it empowers you to do what you want to do, or whether it disempowers you from achieving your goals. NLP offers you the technology to make these fundamental choices.

The technique can be used in many situations. Most training professionals know the power of motivation in any learning situation; if we are highly motivated, we tend to learn better and accomplish more. You now have a device to motivate yourself to almost any degree. By recalling a past experience when you were highly motivated and anchoring that state of mind, you can use it any time you need to be highly motivated for a particular task.

Resources anchoring
You can use the technique to create any resource you wish at will. For example, you may wish to summon up a particular mental *resource*—creativity or enthusiasm—that you have experienced in the past. The process is the same, although you can use it in an ongoing way to recall a state that can be used in many different situations. It may help to summarize the steps:

1 First identify the resource you want.
2 Think back to a specific occasion in your life when you felt this resource—for instance, confidence—and give it a name.
3 Now identify the specific anchors you are going to use in each of the three main representation systems.

K (Kinaesthetic)
A (Auditory)
V (Visual)

For the K modality, think of a physical gesture such as a clenched fist, squeezed fingers—anything, provided it is unique and discreet and you can easily remember it and associate it with the particular resource. For your auditory anchor, think of a word or phrase that evokes the feeling you require. Choose a phrase with a suitable tone that you can say to yourself, such as 'this is no problem'. Then think of a visual image which evokes the feeling of confidence that you want. For example, the actual scene that you record in which you were confident, a specific object or person in that empowering scene, or even some visual metaphor or natural phenomenon that, to you, symbolizes confidence.
4 In your imagination take yourself right back into the experience of, in this case, being confident. Remember where you were, what you were doing, and what you could see, hear and feel around you. Allow yourself to re-live and enjoy the experience as fully as possible.
5 Just as the feeling of confidence is reaching its peak, connect all three anchors—that is, hold the state for a few moments and apply each of the anchors you have decided on. To reinforce all this, you will need to repeat steps 4 and 5 a few times. You can test your success in the process by using the anchors and noting that they access the state you desire.
6 Identify the first thing you might see, hear or feel in any situation in which you would like to respond with greater confidence. It could be the voice of a friend who tends to crush your confidence, or the room in which you have to conduct a regular meeting, or even the feel of sitting in a particular chair. The purpose of identifying this signal is to make sure that you are quickly aware of the need for your chosen state and thus can use your resource anchors to pre-empt a negative state of mind. You can then use your specific anchors—gesture, sound and image—to summon up the state of confidence, or any other state, whenever you wish.

The technique can be applied to any state you can recall and anchor. Choose different anchors for each state so that each has a unique association. If you have difficulty recalling times when you enjoyed a desired state, you can even imagine you are someone else.

We have seen how feelings affect our behaviour in a major way. We may be able to change our behaviour externally, but unless we can somehow change the thought processes associated with that behaviour—in other words, our state of mind—we shall never really change in the long term. That behaviour, and any achievements that follow, will be affected as we revert to old habits supported by feelings and attitudes. Most importantly, you now know how feelings or states of mind are created and how you can, quite literally, change how you feel. This will give you more control, more choices, and a better chance of achieving your outcomes.

8 Beliefs that empower

It has long been established that the feelings and mental attitudes discussed in the previous chapter account for a large part of success in individuals. When these attitudes are so entrenched that they become personal beliefs—beliefs about things, about people and, more particularly, beliefs about ourselves—they have an even greater effect on behaviour and results. In some cases, we will almost argue black is white rather than risk discarding some cherished belief. In fact, the beliefs that impact most on personal achievement are beliefs about ourselves. Each of us has a portfolio of personal beliefs, some of which are positive and some negative. On the positive side you might feel, for instance, that you are 'good with numbers' or 'get on easily with people' or are naturally athletic or fit. On the negative side you might believe you 'can't draw a straight line', that you are disorganized, or that you have no confidence in a public situation, such as giving a speech. Each of these beliefs account for much of your behaviour in the particular area of your life they apply to, and they work in a self-fulfilling way. And it is this self-fulfilling tendency that makes self-belief so powerful—it feeds on itself.

A salesman may 'see himself' as a £20 000 a year salesman, and act and achieve accordingly. Another may see himself as a £100 000 a year salesman, and similarly live out the self-image, achieving the expected outputs. If experience and technical skills are compared, there may be no significant difference between the two professionals. Even the words they use and external behaviour seem to be the same. It is the underlying self-belief that makes all the difference.

This applies in every walk of life. A woman who sees herself as a good public speaker will usually live out the role, accepting any opportunity to undertake speaking engagements and thus further honing her skills and confirming her positive image as an excellent speaker. Conversely, a negative self-image in the same field will be largely self-fulfilling, and actual performance will reinforce the belief. Opportunities to gain experience will be avoided, sometimes in ingenious ways, so even basic experience is forfeited, however senior the executive. Again, in terms of natural abilities and appearance, there may be little difference between the two managers. Their beliefs, however, dictate performance and results. A negative self-image in the area of interpersonal relationships and communication will have a similar all-pervading effect, however irrational the belief may seem to colleagues and close relatives.

These and other aspects of belief will inevitably affect a trainer's performance, notwithstanding extensive training and experience. A person conveniently labelled as a 'round peg in a square hole' might be living out the most irrational self-belief, and be no less fitted to the job than a top performer. As these beliefs extend to every area of our lives, such as the management of time, some operating quite unconsciously, they are probably the biggest single factor in achieving our outcomes. In my experience, additional skill training that goes counter to a strongly held belief not only gives little or no return on the input investment, but can be counter-productive, adding guilt to an already flagging self-esteem. Personal development must therefore address attitudes and beliefs before outward behavioural skills—which usually follow whatever the formal training provision.

The whole process is efficiently self-reinforcing. If you see yourself negatively in one particular area, you tend to *interpret* your behaviour also in that negative way, remembering and accentuating the failings, rather than the successes, when they come. Your interpretation then simply reinforces your belief, so a downward spiral comes into effect, which ensures that you will never excel in that field, nor achieve worthwhile outcomes. Even a success is labelled a 'fluke', or explained away. Conversely, a positive self-image can do absolute wonders for your goal achievement, even when your level of skill, knowledge and experience might not seem to support that positive belief. For present purposes, you would do well to *leave alone* any positive or empowering beliefs about yourself—they are already contributing, no doubt, towards many of your successes. You need, however, to address those disempowering beliefs about yourself which, whatever their origin, are not helping you to achieve your goals today.

An examination of these negative self-beliefs will probably show that they have little rational basis, and this becomes particularly clear when we discuss our beliefs with other people, who can see us more objectively. In most cases, the origins of these self-beliefs go back to childhood. Even a chance remark, especially from a parent or authority figure, can set off the train of thought that produces the negative spiral. In other cases, we simply cannot identify the origin of the negative self-belief. It is almost certain, however, that there is no *rational* physical or mental basis for our self-belief, either in our genetics or early lives.

In trying to change your behaviour to affect your achievements and performance, you need to identify the roles that are played by these feelings, attitudes and beliefs. As beliefs are the most deep-rooted, and clearly have the biggest overall effect on what you do and how you do it, we shall concentrate on these. It is a good idea to select the top few that seem to cause the greatest problems. Once you can identify them and begin to understand the debilitating effect they have on your behaviour and performance, you can then begin to rectify them. Based on our understanding of thought processes, NLP allows you to have some *choice* in how you feel, what your attitudes are and, even more important, what you believe about yourself.

The test of a belief

Once we understand that our self-beliefs are 'negotiable' and not 'carved in stone', we can start questioning and testing them. A good test of a belief, for example, is whether it helps or hinders the achievement of your present-day goals, and whether it is one you consciously choose to have today, or is a vestige of your childhood, or has some irrational origin. Remember that each belief forms a spiral of behaviour. It takes you in a self-fulfilling way in a certain direction, either empowering you or disempowering you. Therefore, unlike changing outward behaviour, which is often short-lived, changing a belief is a wise investment—it has 'leverage'. A single change can bring about many years of increasing empowerment in whole areas of your life. And, however long-standing your beliefs, changing them is no more difficult than tackling a habit of outward behaviour. The process used, however—the technology, if you like—is different, and this is the role played by NLP.

The nature and source of beliefs

Having established the importance of belief in influencing behaviour and subsequent achievement, let us now consider what belief really is and where it comes from. This should enable you to judge better whether current beliefs, that affect your behaviour and performance, are still valid and useful. You can then make some choices, and, using the belief-changing techniques of NLP, make changes for the better.

Environment

Our environment and surroundings in early life play a big part in the system of beliefs that we adopt. We have already seen how important models are in life—we tend to watch and copy people as we go through different stages of our development. When we are surrounded by failure models, we have little positive material on which we can successfully model our own lives. When, on the other hand, we are surrounded by success, achievement and initiative, we will be more inclined to choose successful models and thus achieve more ourselves.

The effect of environment on our achievement may not be obvious, and can be quite subtle. Many people have had a very difficult start in life in terms of material wealth—but somehow they cope and prosper. The day-to-day effect of a poor environment and early education need not take its toll in later achievement. What, however, *does* take its toll is the absence of empowering belief. When our *dreams* are quashed from an early age, because of what we see around us and the influence of 'failure' models, we may be inhibited from developing those dreams. On the other hand, if we believe we can rise above our circumstances, then no environment will be strong enough to hold us back. The impact on our beliefs is the real cost of the environment when it comes to personal goal achievement. If an adverse environment strengthens our belief and resolve, as is sometimes the case, it might actually prove to be an advantage. A single positive influence in our early environment, perhaps a school teacher or relative, can make all the difference.

By emphasizing environment, we are discounting genetic influences. The old nature or nurture question invariably arises, however, when we consider human nature and achievement. But some interesting work has been done in this area. Dr Benjamin Bloom of the University of Chicago studied 100 very successful young musicians, athletes and other students. He was surprised in his research to find that most of these young prodigies did not begin by showing great flashes of brilliance. Instead, most, it transpired, had received careful attention, guidance and support and *then* they began to develop. The belief system they acquired during that early period was what seemed to bring about their later success. This belief, however, only developed when it was nurtured in an appropriate environment, so it seems that environment, rather than genetics, might be the biggest single generator of belief, although not the only one. The very randomness of the environment factor might cause us to question outdated beliefs in later life.

Events   Most people can think back on their lives and clearly recall a few events that have influenced their beliefs and what they are today. It might be a particular achievement at school that gave you great pleasure, or meeting some famous person who greatly influenced you. It could be a great sporting event that you attended, and witnessed what in hindsight was a historic occasion. It seems there is something hit-and-miss about the way events influence and change our lives. But it is clear that the greater the variety of experience we have, the richer will be our basis of personal understanding and belief. As well as the large events which are easily recalled, we tend to be influenced by innumerable small events which exist in the memory but are seldom recalled. These many events, together, help to form our complex system of beliefs and values—what we believe about other people, the world around us, and of course, ourselves.

Knowledge   Another source of belief is knowledge. You can, of course, obtain knowledge from your own direct experience, which is why actual events have such a force in establishing beliefs. But you can also obtain knowledge second-hand, through television, reading, and seeing the world as it is portrayed in different ways by others. Knowledge is one of the best routes by which to escape the boundaries of a limiting environment. Most success stories of people growing up in extreme poverty and hardship have involved their gaining knowledge of the larger world outside, either through reading, meeting other people, or, in due course, through travel. When you *know* something for certain, it changes your belief. So the constant acquisition of knowledge is a major part of your belief system. We live in a knowledge society, and are able to foster beliefs through the knowledge that we acquire. Old and outdated beliefs are discarded as we acquire new knowledge, and new beliefs are born. Every belief, however—old or new—will affect your behaviour and achievements.

Past results   What we have achieved in the past also has a major effect on what we believe about ourselves, both for the present and the future. If you have accomplished something even once, then, with the right attitude, you can believe that you can accomplish it again and again. If you have never accomplished a particular activity or skill, it is much more difficult to believe that you could carry it out in the future. This brings us back to the importance of *doing* in the successful cycle of achievement. Only by doing will we ever know what we can accomplish. In a technical sense, all we need is one successful memory in order to replicate that success over and over again. That memory can form the beginnings of a strong belief system. Each subsequent success reinforces our belief in our own ability.

The results on which you base your present beliefs need not always be achievements in a specific area. If you have achieved almost miraculous deadlines time after time in your working life, you will build up the confidence—that is, the belief in yourself—to achieve impossible deadlines in the future, whatever task you face. So success in one area is readily transferable to success in another, and the more we achieve in different fields, the more we will transfer our positive belief into new and even more challenging areas. It is a good exercise from time to time to list your past achievements. Some of these might have been long forgotten, but as you recall them they can form the basis of successes today and in the future as they affect your belief in yourself as a goal achiever. Some people have accomplished a lot outside the work context, but have not used their strong self-belief in those social or domestic areas to enhance their work performance. Past results, of all sorts, are personal assets that can be invested in future success.

Mental rehearsal   Another source of belief is the imagination or mental rehearsal of the things we want to do. We have already met this as a technique to reinforce a desired outcome and change how we feel. But this happens naturally in any case, and helps to form our beliefs. An ambition that is clearly etched in the imagination, even as a child, becomes a powerful belief that is likely to be fulfilled. We have seen that the brain does not differentiate between a real experience and one that is clearly imagined.

By clearly imagining an activity or behaviour, we, in effect, construct an internal belief system that we can achieve that activity. As far as the brain is concerned, it seems it has *already* carried out the activity successfully, and thus 'believes' it can be done. While we can draw on past successes from time to time, we sometimes face new challenges. By mental rehearsal we experience results in advance, creating the important self-belief . The big advantage of this technique is that you do not have to experience the many failures that are usually associated with a single past success. You can mentally experience success every time, building up a high 'hit rate', and gaining the confidence you need. If, in the past, you could 'see yourself' doing or being something, the chances are that that internal self-image has helped to make you what you are today.

Identifying beliefs that matter

List 10 personal beliefs, five of which are positive (that is, will tend to help you to achieve your present goals) and five negative, or disempowering (that is, will tend to restrict you from getting what you want). Having done this, try to identify the *source* of these beliefs. Are they from your early environment, events you recall, knowledge you have gained, or results you have achieved in the past? This exercise will help to put your beliefs into some perspective. You might discover that some of your negative beliefs have no rational basis whatsoever; they may have been formed in childhood, or influenced by a random event that has no longer validity for your present life, or concern a person you no longer respect. This exercise will help in the process of changing beliefs which are crucial to achieving the goals you want to achieve. Consider also how training and development strategies can be designed to allow for the different belief systems of trainees, and change them where necessary.

Hierarchy of beliefs

When identifying your beliefs you will find that some are very important, those we might call core beliefs, and some are so fundamental that we would die for them. Other beliefs are far more specific, and are readily changeable when we receive new information or when circumstances seem to dictate that we should believe something else. If you tackle a major landscaping job in your garden on time and within budget, and complete some impressive projects at work, you may change what you believe about yourself as an organizer, 'efficient person', or someone who finishes a job they have started. Or you might change your opinion (what you believe) about a friend or colleague. Although not as fickle as feelings, which can change moment by moment, many beliefs do change over a period. Some, however, seem permanent. A belief 'I am a loner', for example, even after a succession of evidence that would prove the contrary, might survive. Similarly a belief about others—that everybody is out to get whatever they can get, or, conversely, that there is some good in everybody—might not change over a decade, seemingly impervious to actual experience or rationale. Therefore, we each have a hierarchy of beliefs—some life and death, and others of lower importance and dispensable. But every belief represents a personal choice, and you are free at any time to discard or amend it.

Beliefs are not mystical things that we can never understand. With a little thought and analysis, as we have just seen, you can usually delve into their origins, or, at worst, determine whether they have any rational basis. You can also decide whether a belief helps or prevents the achievement of your goals. Nor need we be saddled with beliefs as genetic baggage. As we have seen, most of our beliefs have been formed through our own experience and exposure to life, within our own memory. Although many beliefs are deep-rooted, especially after several years of self-fulfilling prophecy, our belief system as such is dynamic, and subject to cycles and feedback as is any other part of human experience.

Starting with the 10 beliefs you have already identified, first consider whether any fit higher beliefs and values. Then think of beliefs that in turn support those you first chose. As an example, a belief 'I'm no good with numbers' might support a wider belief such as 'I'm not good at anything academic' or 'I can't concentrate for long'. But this belief in turn might be supported by 'I never get the budget to balance' or 'I'm hopeless checking my change'. Your interdependent beliefs will then form a hierarchy.

Here are some examples of self-beliefs that may be disempowering:

- I feel awkward in a large social gathering
- I can't draw a straight line
- I'm tone deaf
- I couldn't make a speech if you paid me
- I'm a real loner
- I just can't remember names
- My mind easily goes blank
- I can't concentrate for long
- I know I must look older than I am
- I could never be a boss
- I have a terrible accent
- I am hopeless when it comes to anything academic
- I am a very slow reader
- I am not a healthy person
- I am no good with anything mechanical
- Hardly any clothes really suit me
- People usually take what I say the wrong way
- I easily get tired

- I suppose I am stubborn like my father
- I am never ready on time
- I am prone to accidents.

The self-belief spiral

Belief formation and reinforcement follows a simple spiral. We each start off with basically unlimited potential, to do or achieve or be something. Based upon what you believe about yourself and the situation in hand, you will take action to fulfil that potential. You might decide, for instance, to do nothing because you do not believe you can acquire a certain skill or achieve anything. As in the cybernetic cycle we have already seen, action brings about results, and these results, in turn, reinforce our belief or attitude about ourselves and the world around us. Therefore, people who see little potential for change will produce scant positive action to bring about any worthwhile results. They do not believe it is worth a serious attempt. Their limited attempts and disappointing results will in turn affect their belief or attitude, which in turn restricts their future potential for achievement. This model can therefore be a self-fulfilling prophecy of success where positive action brings about worthwhile results which reinforce a belief in oneself and opens up greater potential for new action and even greater results. Or it can be a downward spiral of failure, when little is attempted, with precious few worthwhile results and a negative belief that it is no longer worth trying.

This belief cycle is fundamental to the learning process. If it is not incorporated into any training design or philosophy, poor results will be almost guaranteed. The wisdom of all this is well established in such phrases as 'success breeds success' and 'failure breeds failure'. But an understanding of the mental and physiological processes involved, together with techniques that can change and reverse the cycle, now enable us to intervene into the learning and goal-achievement process in a way that has not been done before.

In T&D terms, reversing a negative belief cycle is likely to give a very high return on the effort invested, as the process becomes self-fulfilling. No great 'effort' is needed, other than an understanding of our underlying thought processes and of how they can be changed. The change in behaviour happens cybernetically—without conscious effort—in pursuance of an outcome and in line with beliefs and values. Therefore, although less tangible than outward behaviour, self-belief forms the basis of all behaviour and cannot be ignored if long-term change—outputs rather than inputs—is the training objective.

NLP belief change pattern

We have seen that belief is a big factor in what we do and, in turn, what we achieve. According to NLP, belief—like attitude and feelings—is just a way of thinking; a mental strategy for relating to the world around us. As we have also seen, beliefs can be both acquired and discarded over time, and this usually happens unconsciously as we encounter different life situations, gain new knowledge, and mature. But we also saw that beliefs can be consciously changed. Here is an exercise that will help you to change any belief pattern. You can use it to simply and gently transform limiting beliefs into deeply felt empowering beliefs which will create a sense of self-worth and enable you to master all sorts of situations.

1   Identify a belief you now hold that limits you in some way. For instance, the belief might be 'I'm no good at public speaking', or 'I'm no good with numbers'. Choose one which, if changed, could open up real opportunities for you to achieve more during the next few weeks and months.

2   Identify what you would rather believe—that is, your *preferred* belief—and state this in a positive form (remember the tests of a good outcome we covered in Chapter 3). Complete an ecology check—ensure that any change will respect your family, friends and work colleagues.

3   Now create a label on a sheet of paper for each of six imaginary locations of belief change.

   (a)   Current belief
   (b)   Open to doubt
   (c)   Museum of old beliefs
   (d)   Preferred belief
   (e)   Open to belief
   (f)   Call this the special or sacred place.

4   Place these labels on the floor in a clockwise direction as though they were places round an imaginary dinner table, so that you can move physically from one to the other.

5   Next, establish some sort of anchor for each of the six labels and locations. As you physically step from one to the other, think of a vivid experience from your life that fits each description. You should easily be able to identify your *current belief*—this is the one you would like to change—and imagine yourself in a situation that illustrates this. Then think of a time in the past when you were *open to doubt*—your belief was not strong, doubts had crept in. The belief in *open to doubt* might relate to you and your abilities, another person, or even an ideology. For the *museum of old beliefs*, think back to something that you once held as a belief, but no longer believe is true. You will probably think of several dating back to childhood, but some may have been discarded recently. Your *preferred belief* is the one you would now like to adopt, so, for the moment, you need to imagine that you believe what you want to believe—or perhaps what it would be like to be another person who you know holds the desired belief. The *open to belief* label will

be anchored by some experience in the past when you were open to believe—that is, you had not yet formed a new belief, but your understanding and the facts of a situation made you open to changing what you then believed. Try to think of an actual situation when you were in this particular state of mind. Finally, for the *special or sacred place*, think of a belief that you would never discard—something which is so important that it is, to you personally, a matter of life and death. Complete one round of the labels and, in each position, try to vividly recollect a situation and state of mind that illustrates each of the different locations.

6 Standing in the *current belief* location, experience again your limiting belief.

7 Taking this limiting belief with you, step from *current belief* into *open to doubt*, and, recalling the earlier experience of open to doubt, notice how you are now doubting that limiting belief.

8 Now take your doubted belief and step into the *museum of old beliefs*. Recollect an old discarded belief, feel what it is like to discard your doubted belief and leave it in the *museum of old beliefs*.

9 Having left that belief behind in the *museum of old beliefs*, step into your *preferred belief* location and experience again your preferred belief. Imagine yourself fully believing this new belief, and enjoy how it feels.

10 Now physically move on from the *preferred belief* into the *open to belief* location, and feel yourself again being completely open to believing this is true. Then take your preferred belief and step into the *special or sacred place*. Put your new belief alongside your current sacred beliefs and make it very important to you.

11 Finish the exercise by feeling your now very special and sacred preferred belief as you step back into the current belief location. You will now no longer hold this current belief. It has been transformed, gently, step by step, into the belief that will be empowering for you.

You will need to exercise some imagination in this technique. Moving from one physical location to another—however silly it seems—actually helps you to make the transition into each state of mind. It makes neurological sense. You are getting to know parts of yourself of which you are not usually conscious, and some of the rules for doing this do not sit well with the left, conscious side of your brain. By doing the exercise you will also gain more practice in recalling memories and, in particular, feelings. Being able to recognize, recall and use your various states of mind for present, positive purposes is in itself an important skill.

Systemic belief assessment

There are other approaches to changing beliefs. This one attempts to bring your beliefs into line with a specific outcome. It also helps to identify feelings and other beliefs that might interfere with your outcome—such as whether you feel you deserve to achieve it—even though these may not at first be at a conscious level.

1 Identify some outcome you would like to achieve.
2 Say aloud each of the statements below, rating your degree of confidence on a scale of 1 to 5; with 1 being the lowest, and 5 being the highest degree of belief.

   (a) My goal is desirable and worth it.
   (b) It is possible to achieve my goal.
   (c) What I have to do in order to achieve my goal is appropriate and ecological.
   (d) I have the abilities necessary to achieve my goal.
   (e) I deserve to achieve my goal.

3 Review your ratings and your responses, then ask which of the issues you have discovered are relevant to achieving your outcome. What can you do about it? Are you ready to change a belief?

Verbal frames for limiting belief statements

As we have already seen, we are not always conscious of our limiting beliefs. But they can often be elicited by using such verbal patterns as: 'If I get what I want, then...'. This may remind you of the ecology check used for clarifying goals. A positive intention is identified which might conflict with a different intention (for example, a desire to be liked, and a desire to be single-minded and assertive), each with its own goals. The ecology check seeks to identify both inner conflicting goals, and also any conflict with other people's goals (perhaps a member of your family) that you also hold as important.

Use the following verbal frames to help identify limiting beliefs and incongruent goals. If necessary, change the words around to make the patterns useful for a particular belief.

- Getting what I want would mean ...
- ... causes me to stay the way I don't want to be
- Getting what I want will make ...
- I must stay the way I don't want to be because ...
- I can't get what I want because ...
- It is not possible for me to get what I want because ...
- I am not capable of getting what I want because ...
- I'll never get better because ...
- I'll always have this problem because ...
- It is wrong to want to be better because ...
- I don't deserve to get what I want because ...

Beliefs and outcomes

Hopefully the outcome tests we used in Chapter 3 will separate the outcomes you expect to happen from those you do not really believe will happen. Belief is central to goal fixing as well as all subsequent behaviour. Sometimes the process of goal clarification, and more particularly visualizing it, reinforces your expectancy and belief that you will achieve it. And this applies to a dream holiday, getting a promotion, or anything else—belief can be created and nurtured.

Outcomes are essential, but they will differ in importance, urgency and in just how we feel about them. However we rationally prioritize them, the main factors helping us to succeed are (a) our belief that they are within our reach, and (b) the motivation we bring to them. One goal might drive you to achieve an impossible deadline, while another might stay at the bottom of your mental in-tray. In terms of your state of mind, one might be a wish or pipedream, and the other a strong desire.

Changing wishes into wants

The goal clarification test was designed to weed out or at least amend outcomes that are not well formed—including wishes. But the difference between a want and a wish is to do with our mental strategy—how we think about the outcome. The sort of techniques we have already met can also be applied to outcomes—in effect to change a wish into a want. You were not aware of these techniques (involving the representation systems and submodalities covered in Chapter 4) when you set your outcomes at the beginning. But you are now ready to change what you believe about any outcome to make it stronger. This is more than a semantic exercise, although it does indeed help if you express your goals in words that are unequivocal and specific. This process makes the necessary internal changes that turn wishes into wants, and thus become outcomes that are more likely to be achieved. This technique is described assuming that you have a female partner, but you can also do it yourself.

1 Ask your partner to think of something she wishes for. Determine the main submodalities of the visual, auditory and kinaesthetic representations of her wish, by asking questions. Keep a check on her external physiology, which often gives clues as to what is going on inside. Ask her to describe how she thinks about her wish, and make a note of any key words she uses. We are not concerned about the content of the wish, but rather the characteristics of the images that the wish conjures up—the submodalities. So do not ask what the wish is, but just get descriptions of how she thinks about it. She might picture her wish, for instance, and you can elicit the characteristics of the visual images.
2 Now ask your partner to think of something similar that she really wants, a strong desire rather than a wish, and go through the same exercise again. Notice once more the key words she uses in any descriptions, and her physiology, as well as all the specific descriptions of submodalities as she imagines this want.

3 Then elicit from your partner how these two experiences, the wishing and the wanting, differ. Again, you are not concerned with the content, but are looking for possibly two main differences between the submodalities of the two experiences. You may find it necessary to take your partner again through her representation of the experiences. Make a note particularly of the differences between the submodalities using the checklist you used earlier.

4 When you have at least two submodality differences to work on, ask your partner to think of the content of what she was wishing for, but then to change the two critical submodalities that you have identified from a wanting visualization. By switching the submodalities—the *want* characteristics to replace the *wish* characteristics—the wish becomes a better, and more motivating, outcome.

5 Test what you have done by asking what differences she now notices as she thinks about what she was wishing for. How does she feel now about this wish? Keep observing her physiology, tone of voice, etc., as this will often let you know that she has now adopted a want in place of a wish.

Changing just one belief can result in quite dramatic changes in behaviour, but changing a self-belief is likely to have more 'leverage' in changing behaviour than changing a belief about a specific outcome. A belief that 'I am not a natural salesperson', for example, when reversed, can result in a sales performance improvement that no amount of technical training could produce. Similarly, in the case of a trainer, a self-belief that 'I am not very good in up-front situations', when changed, can turn an otherwise mediocre trainer into an outstanding 'up-front' presenter. This is the power of self-image, which, through these NLP techniques, can now be changed. You can choose what to believe about yourself—what you are as well as what you can achieve.

9 Changing behaviour

The link between what we do and the results we achieve has long been established. If you can take control of what you do or how you behave in its minutest detail, then you can certainly take control of your goals and how to achieve them. It all pertains to behaviour. What is also clear, however, is that every behaviour is preceded by a thought. It does not happen in a vacuum; there is an intention, a purpose, a will, that moves us in the direction of achieving our goal. We might be trying to gain pleasure or get away from pain, or both, but in every case our behaviour is purposeful. Therefore, in order to begin to take control of what you do, you need to both understand and learn to take control of how you think or how you perceive things.

Referring back to one of our very first analogies, you need to get to know your own personal map and be able to change it at will to bring about your present purposes. Getting to know yourself better involves understanding the *process* of thinking. We have learned, for instance, about the way the two brain hemispheres process thoughts differently. We have also learned about modalities or representation systems and their many submodalities. Once we have a language of basic thought processes, we can begin to 'think about thinking' and identify and analyse our thoughts in a way that will help us. We can now express these thoughts, upon which our behaviour is based, in terms that we and others can understand. We can describe visual images, sounds or feelings, for example. And we learn that a certain visual image or the sound of a certain voice can make us feel in a certain way, and this affects our behaviour. Therefore, with an understanding of the processes that determine how we feel, and our attitudes, and an awareness of the raw material—the content—we can start doing something about our thinking, just as we can do something about our physical fitness or diet.

Behaviour then follows thinking as surely as night follows day: 'Whatsoever a man thinketh in his heart, so is he' is the timeless truth. You have now learned how to control feelings and change beliefs. In this chapter we shall go a little further in translating this new control into behaviour that brings the outputs we want.

Treating behaviour as a problem

NLP is an excellent approach to solving problems, and any behaviour that we would do better without—is hindering us rather than helping us to achieve our goals—can be subject to problem-solving treatment. Some of the reframing techniques we met in Chapter 6 started with what we call a 'problem-statement'. We then applied various perspectives and different lines of enquiry to see the problem in a different light. In some cases, you will find that what seems to be a problem initially is nothing of the sort, and can be turned into an opportunity or a blessing in disguise. In other cases the very basis changes, and you find yourself dealing with an entirely different problem. Sometimes the process seems to take you backwards, and the real problem is bigger, but in reality you are getting ever closer to the achievement of your goals. By tackling the wrong problem, you are simply delaying achievement of your eventual purpose. By beginning to ask the right questions and identifying the true problem, at very worst you get closer to reaching your objective.

Many problems relate to other people and our relationships with them. One of the advantages of treating a behaviour change as a problem is that we start off by accepting or 'owning' the problem ourselves. We thus take responsibility for changing our behaviour, rather than instinctively blaming the other person, as is often the case. This is a sound philosophy for achieving your outcomes. You will recall the presupposition that the nature of communication is to do with the results it brings about. While you might spend much time finding reasons to blame the person with whom you were communicating, in the final analysis it is your purposes that you want to fulfil by the communication—to inform, impress, warn, persuade, etc. That is to achieve *your* objective. You will also remember the importance of your 'own part' in the goal clarification test in Chapter 3, and this further reinforces the importance of owning your goals *and* the obstacles that lie in their path.

It makes sense, therefore, to treat behaviour you want to change as your problem. In some situations you might indeed find that you have to change the other person, and there is plenty within NLP to help you to do this. But the starting point is yourself, and by clearly defining the behaviour you wish to change in the form of a problem-statement, it then becomes amenable to the several techniques we have already used. We can for instance, apply the Sleight of Mouth technique, and thus have a dozen or more different angles at which to view this problem behaviour. It is almost certain that, having done this test, we will see the situation rather differently. It follows from that that we will tend to behave differently because of our different perception.

You can choose almost any behaviour and apply this problem-solving strategy to it. In a training context, there is a very common and not always recognized tendency not to listen. As teachers, we intervene rather too quickly. Of course we are all aware of the textbook theory which encourages listening skills, but nevertheless these habits can be very long-standing, and the bad listener is the last to realize his or her shortcomings.

The Sleight of Mouth technique would elicit lots of angles on such a problem. It would pin-point, for example, each of us individually as the problem holder, and perhaps question whether we have a reasonable or jaundiced view of ourselves. Perhaps our family or professional colleagues would in no way agree that we are bad listeners, but somehow we are tarred with some historical perceptual brush that makes us think we are. This self-image, in its self-fulfilling way, can be the real problem. When the Sleight of Mouth tool moves round to the chunking down option, we might ask in what particular respects do we consider ourselves to be bad listeners. In every situation, or just in certain cases? We might then be able to diagnose some connections between our apparently poor listening skills and the immediate circumstances, and learn much from this. Or our poor listening skills might be confined to certain people, boiling down to a relationship, and again related to our personal map—how we perceive the person and the situation. Upward chunking might ask whether this apparent poor listening skill applies far more widely than in a training context. In other words, we have a bigger personal issue to resolve. At the end of the exercise, we shall probably be faced with many new angles on our problem, and might well have to forget the issue for an incubation period to allow ideas to settle down in our mind. It might also be a very good basis to discuss the situation with a close colleague or relation. But one thing is almost certain, that the behaviour that we are seeking to understand and amend will change to some degree in the process. In some cases, where a real insight has been opened through the reframing process, the change in behaviour will be quite dramatic and will be readily seen by others. In effect we become 'a different person'. In other cases the change will be gradual, as we become more and more aware of ourselves, fall into bad habits less and less frequently, and choose how we think and behave. So any behavioural problem is subject to the reframing techniques already described. The 'problem' might be just that the behaviour is not achieving the outcome we want, and we need to think of another method of achieving it.

A major area of behaviour, as we have seen, concerns other people, and in particular ongoing relationships. One of the techniques we met in Chapter 6 which has been used very successfully in this area is the Points of View technique. List any behaviour patterns that you would like to change that fall in this area of personal relationships, frame each one as a sentence as suggested, then apply the various words to form the reframed sentences. Check to see if this brings about any insights into your personal situation. By doing this exercise, even if no 'eureka' seems to emerge, you will have changed forever your perceptual map of this little part of your world. That is, you will have a better relationship and see things differently *vis-à-vis* the other person. Your perceptual map is, of course, your blueprint of reality and what causes you to behave as you do.

Behaviour and positive intentions

One of the NLP presuppositions we met in Chapter 2 is that there is always a positive intention, or some purpose, behind any behaviour. Therefore, one approach to changing behaviour is, first, to establish the purpose behind it. In many cases you should be able to identify several possible intentions which underlying any undesirable behaviour. In some cases they might be for very logical reasons—at least logical to you. In other cases the intentions may not make much sense, but can at least be identified. The listening problem illustrates this. Perhaps you are not impressed with the quality of what you are listening to and decide to save valuable training time by moving the situation forward. Perhaps you feel that by giving the information required, you can shorten the long process of questioning. Or you might feel that what is being said is irrelevant in the particular learning context. Each of these 'positive intentions' on your part will make some sense to some degree, at least to you. We might even be able to find positive intentions when addressing a far more controversial behaviour such as smoking, or a habit we want to stop. However, in other cases the intention is not nearly as clear, especially on the part of the person with the behaviour problem. It operates from an unconscious level.

We shall meet other NLP techniques that help us to elicit these positive intentions. For the moment try to relate your behaviour to intentions, then think about different behaviour that might allow you to achieve these intentions in a more acceptable way. Do the same in the case of other people's behaviour—assume positive intentions, seek to identify them, and find better ways (better to them) of achieving their intentions. It is important to understand that our purposes and intentions control all our behaviour. If we can discover the source of these purposes, we can begin to change our behaviour.

In addition to treating behaviour as a problem and applying creative problem-solving techniques, it can also be viewed as a natural expression of a positive intention. But the desired intention is the personal driver, and there may well be choices in how to achieve the outcome.

Unconscious competence

Most of our behaviour happens when we are not conscious of what we are doing. According to some researchers, well over 90 per cent of all our behaviour is controlled from a subconscious level. Most of us are quite familiar with having undertaken an activity without remembering anything about it. This can range from getting dressed in the morning to undertaking a long car drive across country. During these periods our mind might well be occupied with other matters. We are conscious, of course, but our consciousness is not directed to the activity we are then undertaking automatically. The activity itself has become a habit; we have done it so many times. We no longer need to *try* to do it, or give higher level thought to the task. As we have already seen, this seems to apply in all sorts of sporting situations or where we are involved in physical activities. Once the brain has registered a physical activity, we can then carry it out in a more or less automatic way. In fact, most sports people find that when they think about the activity in a conscious way, their performance is reduced rather than enhanced. The same often applies to driving, cooking, or any other learned skill. It would seem, therefore, that conscious thought is given over to, perhaps, the strategy of the game rather than the automatic functions of the activities themselves.

This idea of unconscious behaviour is very important in NLP. It has been well established that excellence in behaviour needs to be brought to this unconscious competence level. That is, we need to get beyond the stage at which we are thinking about each and every part of any activity. It needs to become natural and instinctive. It then follows that the more of our many behaviours that we can carry out in this unconscious way, the better will be our overall performance. We can reserve our conscious mind, which, if you like, represents the tip of the thinking iceberg, for immediate pressing considerations, *real* problems, or further learning.

Often the idea of unconscious activity is confined to simple tasks like dressing, cleaning your teeth and so on. But we have already seen how we can undertake a long car journey with all its complexity and even potential danger and the whole operation is controlled somewhere below the conscious level. As you start watching out for people who seem to achieve goals and exhibit personal excellence, you will observe this kind of unconscious behaviour more and more. A behaviour which to some people would seem extraordinarily difficult or even impossible would be relegated to unconscious competence by other people. We marvel at top performers in any area of life, from sports to art and music. But we often find that they are not only unconscious of what they are doing, but, for this very reason, find it difficult to pass on the secrets of their success. This is where NLP helps. We now have a common language of thought, and can begin to elicit those strategies or patterns of thought that are used in excellent behaviour. While there is no substitute for the physical practice that most skills demand, the thinking strategies are what seem to make the critical difference, and these can be modelled. The idea of unconscious competence is also an important part of how we learn new skills, and this is covered in Chapter 10.

Mental rehearsal and self-image

We have already met the idea of mental rehearsal, and this fits in with the idea of unconscious competence in behaviour. Unconscious competence applies, as we have seen, at many levels, from the most mundane of tasks to a very complex and extended set of behaviours such as undertaking a long car journey or even running a training programme.

Levels of mental rehearsal

Using a golf analogy, at one level we can mentally rehearse a swing. The mental rehearsal acts as a blueprint which the physical body and nervous system follow. Any interference of the left brain—the conscious, critical part of our thinking—will undermine our ability at this level. If we can do something well once, then physically we can do it well again. The important thing is to adopt the mental strategy which ensures the right instructions to bring about the same behaviour.

At the next level, mental rehearsal can be applied very successfully to the whole game of golf or any other game. The principle of clear visualization can apply just as effectively to a range of activities, or a whole game, as it can to an individual stroke. It can and should certainly include the winning accolades, the receiving of the medal or some award at the end of the activity—that is, the goal having been fully reached. Chris Lloyd Evert, the tennis player, besides visualizing the individual aspects of her game, would visualize the whole game incorporating the opponent. Even the specific tactics and strategy of the game would be pre-visualized as part of her mental preparation. Using this approach, the whole of the game then potentially becomes one of unconscious competence, or of excellence. Therefore, a complex series of activities, such as giving a dinner party, running a training programme or managing a company, can be brought largely to the level of unconscious competence—the skills are carried out instinctively and 'without trying'. This apparent ease is one of the hallmarks of personal excellence and true professionalism.

There is one further level to which mental rehearsal can apply, and this is even more important than the previous two levels: the issue that has most influence on performance is how we see ourselves—that is, our self-image, as a person or in a particular field of activity or behaviour.

- Do I see myself as a top golfer or a hacker?
- Do I see myself as a champion, or as a number 25?
- In the sales area, do I see myself as a top salesperson or is this not really me?
- Can I see myself as a boss?

If we harbour a negative self-image in the *overall* area of behaviour—for instance, as a 'trainer', 'consultant' or 'scratch golfer'—then whatever our visualization at the two previous levels, we shall be drawn towards our negative self-image. This will result in internal conflict and, in effect, we shall be living a lie.

Human excellence has to involve *being* as well as *doing*. We must see ourselves and imagine ourselves as being what we want to be as well as doing what we want to achieve. The same mental rehearsal technique can be used, but it will embrace wider aspects of our behaviour and lifestyle. A soccer player who sees himself as a creditable fourth division player might accomplish a lot within the fourth division context. At the level of the shot at goal, or the brilliant header, or even in the game overall, he may similarly excel. At some level, however, his limited self-image will take its toll. A series of good results that might indicate promotion next season might mysteriously come to an end as the team does not seem able to cope with the idea of the higher league. This is usually reflected in several of the individuals and thus the team as a whole. A person might be able *to* do the part, but cannot cope with *being* the part, to which is where higher self-beliefs become effective.

To change our behaviour we need to understand it on these different levels. Mental rehearsal and reframing generally can apply at each level, but we adapt the technique to meet the individual situation. Our visualization will be directed differently if we are directing our attention towards our overall self-image. The soccer player will need to see and hear and feel the experiences of being a third division player, not just of the activities of scoring a goal or winning an individual match. His visualization will inevitably embrace domestic and social life, all of which will be affected by his success as a *person*, rather than just in an activity. In real life you are a total person, and powerful visualization captures this reality. All of this is possible because nothing is outside the power of the human imagination. As we reach the higher level of self-image, however, many more of our characteristics are brought into the behaviour or activity. Referring back to the goal clarification exercise, there also needs to be far greater consideration of the ecology of our purposes and goals. How would it affect the rest of your life if you reached the top echelons of your career or profession or hobby or sport? These questions can be explored by mental visualization, and during this process you may discover conflicts of personal intention.

Therefore, the process can be used to test our goals and desires, as well as to reinforce those we have already decided upon. One seminar delegate, having clearly visualized some idyllic, long holiday abroad, changed his mind about it. Having pre-lived the experience, he found it boring after a few days. In this respect, mental rehearsal can also be an inexpensive way to test a goal or dream.

These levels of behaviour, and the importance of self-image, do not just apply in a sporting context. You can use the analogy directly in a training context. At the level of the golf stroke, you would use mental rehearsal techniques to improve any aspect of your performance in the training situation, from practising a prepared speech, to using the overhead projector in an effective and skilful way. The many actual activities that a professional trainer undertakes can be broken down, and each one well prepared by mental rehearsal. In some situations prior visualization is more effective than actual experience as you need not practise failure—just success—and unnecessary negative brain memories are avoided. And in any event actual success memories can be strengthened by frequent recall. The game of golf might then be compared with a programme, or course of training, in which case you would visualize not just individual activities but the final outcome, including any review, and the response of delegates. This level, of course, supports the first level, and you eliminate incongruence between a series of excellent behaviours and what might still be an unsuccessful overall programme outcome. Finally, in your visualization at the seminar or event level you will take account, for example, of adequate breaks to allow for concentration span, reviews, time for questions and free-wheeling interaction, the 'housekeeping' arrangements, and the whole social side of the programme. All these will contribute towards higher level programme goals. Excellent lower level activities—even adhering scrupulously to an agenda—might be found to be in conflict when the higher goal is considered.

But the third level is vital. If you do not 'see yourself' as a professional trainer, a confident public speaker, an 'up-front person', gregarious, or whatever, your self-image might well be disempowering in the context of your training goals. It could have the effect of negating not only your actual skills but even the mental rehearsal that you might use to try to improve them. In other words, there will still be incongruence between what you do and what you are. Returning to the golf analogy, it takes more than a perfect swing, even a mentally rehearsed one, to make a championship golfer. Visualization must also apply at the higher level.

The big question remains, of course, whether we can do anything about what we actually are, as this seems to impinge on our personality, and even genetics. But, as we saw earlier, any investigation into our self-images in different areas of life will probably result in them being exposed as quite irrational; that is, there is no strong genetic or environmental reason why most people cannot excel in a behaviour and reach the top of their career, profession or sport. The limitations are in the mind—in the way we think, and in particular in the way that we see ourselves in that area—our self-image. At this third level we are dealing with beliefs, and these are sometimes difficult to change even when we want to change them. These beliefs are not so much about the world or the cosmos, but about ourselves, supported, no doubt, by hundreds of hard disk memories of 'failures'. But, as we saw in the previous chapter, if you were to recall things you believed—even very strongly—5, 10 or 20 years ago, you could probably compile a list of things that you no longer believe. Similarly, there are things that you believe today that you did not believe then. Our beliefs very often change, although the changes are sometimes difficult to recognize in the short term. NLP gives you control over your beliefs, puts environment and genetics in their place and allows belief to be a positive power towards achieving your present goals. You become the master of your thoughts and behaviour.

Excuses

Every behaviour is 'interpreted' by a sort of inner interpreter, and the interpretation of our behaviour affects future behaviour. In NLP terms, we make *excuses* for our behaviour. For instance, if some activity conforms to your self-belief in that area, your interpretation reinforces that belief. You might say, 'That's just me', or 'I find that quite easy' or 'It comes naturally'. When, however, behaviour is contrary to a self-belief, we are likely to think or say, 'That's not like me' or 'It was a fluke' or 'That rarely happens'. Each interpretation reinforces the self-belief and thus further influences future behaviour. According to Dr Martin Seligman, this 'inner interpreter' has three different language dimensions: time, place and person.

Time

Excuses can be permanent or temporary. For instance, you might say, 'It's all over; things will never work out', or, conversely, '*That* chance is passed, *it* didn't work the way I'd planned'. Temporary interpretations need not affect your self-belief. They are put behind you. Permanent excuses tend to use words like 'never' or 'always', which leave no room for change.

Place

Excuses can be either pervasive or specific. Examples of pervasive language are: 'All bosses are just interested in themselves', 'He is a failure' or 'I can't draw'. Examples of specific language, on the other hand, might be 'He (that boss) is just interested in himself', 'I didn't do what I had planned in this situation' or 'I didn't sell to that particular customer'. Interpreting a behaviour in the context of a specific situation or time is less likely to affect how you feel, and what you believe about yourself to the extent that a pervasive interpretation does. Interpreting it as pervasive, and likely to recur, however, does tend to affect us, and will influence future behaviour in a self-fulfilling way.

Person

Excuses can be either personal or impersonal. For example, you might say 'I'm to blame' or 'I'm just disorganized'. Alternatively, you might say 'The situation is difficult' or 'There is just too much to organize' or 'We were overtaken by events'. When we de-personalize an action, we do not feel as strongly about it. Even though we have *done* something, we do not interpret it as being because of what we *are*.

If you think about your many actions throughout the day, you should be able to give an interpretation to each of them (I did so-and-so because ...). This will reflect your self-beliefs and values as well as your perception of the specific behaviour. Every interpretation—or 'excuse'—will in turn affect your future behaviour. We live by our excuses, creating congruence in what we do. But interpretations are just mental strategies or programmes—and form part of our personal map of reality. As such they are changeable—open to negotiation. The insidious but well-meaning, self-fulfilling inner interpreter of all our behaviour can therefore become an ally or servant rather than a master.

Understanding and using your inner interpreter

By understanding and controlling the way you interpret your behaviour you can change your attitude to different areas of activity: (a) becoming optimistic in situations when you would normally have been pessimistic, or (b) becoming more positive. We need to understand this process of interpreting our behaviour—of making excuses. In effect, we need to get to know, then positively control, our 'inner interpreter'. Here is an exercise to help you. You will need to suspend your rational, left-brain logic, which is out of its depth when dealing with the unconscious side of your thinking, and use some right-brain imagination.

1   Think back to a time when things did not turn out the way you would have hoped. Be quite specific.
2   As you think back, ask yourself, 'How do I explain this action and the result? Why didn't it turn out the way I wanted?', and listen attentively to your inner interpreter, writing down what seems to come into your mind.
3   Repeat the first two steps, but this time using other events, perhaps linking them with some emotional content.
4   Have a look at the explanations you have written as your interpretations or 'excuses'. What is similar between them? Now check them for permanence of time, pervasiveness of place, and personal responsibility, referring if necessary to the examples used above.
5   Now rewrite your explanations to make them more optimistic. For example, if they are permanent, make them temporary. If they are all-pervasive, make them specific. If they are personal, make them impersonal.
6   Notice where in mental space these voices or interpretations seemed to come from. Notice whether they all came from a similar direction.
7   As you listen to this inner interpreter and become familiar with the voice and the sort of things it is saying, realize that this is an important part of your subconscious, and helps to explain how you see and understand the world. Be thankful that this interpreter is there and is concerned with your welfare.
8   Now that you are aware of the positive intention behind your behaviours and that your inner critic or interpreter is on your side, update your explanations with more optimistic and useful ones—

excuses that will be empowering rather than disempowering in the future.

9 Now imagine the voice of your inner interpreter moving its location to your elbow and taking on the sound of a newscaster. You are free to change it to any kind of voice—maybe the high-pitched voice of a child. When you hear this voice again, imagine it coming from your thumb, and this time offer to your critic the explanations you thought of for creating greater optimism and empowerment. Then listen as your inner interpreter takes these on board and provides you with plenty of examples of mastering the skill or situation you are concerned about. Notice how you feel when you hear this change of explanations.

10 Finally, let your inner interpreter move back up your arm and shoulder to your head. Give it the sort of voice that you find most attractive and compelling, as this is the tone of voice that will have most influence upon you.

Once you are familiar with the technique, think of other past behaviour that might benefit from it. A general attitude will usually pervade work and personal life, so the more cases you use, the more apparent will your inner interpreter's working methods become. But, more importantly, you will see how simple it can be to intervene in what are usually irrational 'excuses' made 'without thinking'. You do not *have* to change your interpretation of any action, but you are *free* to do so. And this freedom gives you choice and control that you would not otherwise have had.

Inner team building pattern

When we looked at clarifying our goals in Chapter 3, we saw the importance of what was called ecology. We also learned that behind every behaviour there is a positive intention. We are not always conscious, of course, of our intentions. And they may be, moreover, in conflict with each other. These conflicting intentions have to be reconciled if we are to pursue clear, unambiguous outcomes. In effect, each of us is not just one person but many, each vying for its own outcomes. We even use phrases like 'one part of me wants to do it, and another does not'. There is what may be called an inner team, and it is important to make this team work together, pulling in the direction *you* decide.

Here is an NLP pattern for building this congruence in your inner team. You will quickly realize the idea behind it and you may wish to amend it to make it more sensible to you. However, you will again have to call upon all your powers of imagination, so try to free yourself of all interruptions and 'suspend judgement' while you are doing the exercise. You will be bringing to awareness different parts of yourself. One part, for example, might be the supreme diplomat, always correct socially, and courteous. Another part might be blunt and a little rude. One part seems to have endless patience, say with children or in a hobby. Another part has a short fuse. And so on. These are just examples, but we each have many parts to our character, even though most of the time we are not conscious of them. Each of these parts can usually be traced to memories in which you see yourself acting out the part. They reflect the different positive intentions we have, and the conflicts of ecology in our behaviour. Think first about these different parts of you—helpful and unhelpful, public face and private face, empowering and disempowering—each (according to the presupposition we met earlier) pursuing some positive intention on your behalf.

1 Close your eyes and imagine going to some place in nature where you feel very relaxed and comfortable. Then imagine a table with six chairs round it.

2 Ask your unconscious mind for two parts of yourself that you really *enjoy* to come forward. When they arrive, welcome them as they take their seats at the table.

3 Now ask your unconscious mind for two parts of yourself that you find *useful* or *practical* to come forward. When they arrive, welcome them as they take their seats at the table, and introduce everyone.

4 Ask your unconscious mind for two parts of yourself that you particularly *dislike* and with which you are unhappy, and similarly welcome them as they join.

5 Now say to all your guests, 'Please tell me, who here feels the most misunderstood?' and ask the one who responds: 'What is your positive purpose, your positive intention for me, a gift you want to bring me?' Listen carefully to the answer. Notice that the others hear, understand and appreciate the importance of this particular guest's gift. For example, a blunt, rude part might feel it is being truthful and 'calling a spade a spade,' and 'cannot stand hypocrisy'. A short fuse part might feel it is expressing itself frankly and openly, without any social cover up, and that this is better than suppressing issues. The reason may be to get attention, to appear strong, or just to 'get things off my chest'. These are interpretations, or excuses, and expose intentions, or purposes.

6 Then say to the remaining five parts, who among you feels the most misunderstood? Ask the one who responds: 'What is your positive purpose and the gift you want to bring to me?' Again listen to the answer, and notice that the rest of the guests understand and appreciate the importance of this guest's gift.

7 Repeat the process with the remaining four, then three, parts of your team.

8 When there are just two parts remaining say, 'I welcomed the other parts to this table. Please tell me, one at a time, the gift that you bring me', and listen carefully to their answers. Notice that the others understand and appreciate the importance of the gifts that these parts bring.

9 Finally, watch as the six parts create a circle of gifts by holding hands

with each other, then let the table fade away. Stand in the middle of this circle of gifts, allowing the inner team to merge somewhere inside you.

All this is highly subjective, and some people have great difficulty in imagining inner happenings, much less real personalities. However, when you have had some practice in recognizing and manipulating modalities and submodalities, you will find it much easier to recognize even the most subtle inner senses. You will be able to communicate with yourself in a way that perhaps you have not imagined possible. This particular pattern allows you to recognize the many parts within you, but, more particularly, it seeks to reconcile different desires and intentions, and might help explain unwanted behaviour. Typically, after carrying out the exercise—and you can do this several times as you become familiar with the pattern—you will experience a sense of wholeness and confidence as you realize that these inner parts of you are on your side—they are you—and want to bring about your welfare.

Turning your actions into empowering beliefs

We have already seen how beliefs and attitudes affect our behaviour, but this is part of a two-way process. Our actions also create beliefs. Depending on your interpretation of your actions, the beliefs formed can be either empowering or disempowering. So here is another pattern that will help you to turn actions into empowering beliefs.

1 Think of something you would like to believe about yourself, but which you are not quite sure is true.
2 State this desired belief in a positive form. This is similar to the goal clarification exercise when we turned outcomes into a positive mode. Check also that your desired belief is one you can do something about yourself, and is not dependent wholly on other people, or circumstances outside your control. Then do an ecology check to make sure the new belief is respectful of your family, friends, work colleagues, etc.
3 Ask yourself what sort of things a person with this desired belief would instinctively do. Imagine and make a list of all sorts of actions that match the belief.
4 Think of some particular time and place in the future when you would like to have this belief.
5 From your list, select some action that is evidence of your desired belief and would be appropriate for the specific future time and place you have chosen.
6 Now visualize yourself in this future situation, doing the chosen action. First, watch the whole future scene as if on a movie screen, with you carrying out the actions. You might need to do this two or three times to ensure that the whole scene is clear and positive.
7 Now start the scene again from the beginning, but this time stepping

right into it as though you were part of it—seeing through your own eyes, and hearing and feeling everything around you through your own senses. Particularly notice your feelings when you carry out this activity according to your desired belief. Say out loud your new belief with conviction as you carry on through the scene to the end.

8 Now repeat steps 4 to 7 a few more times. You can select different appropriate actions from the list you made to illustrate your desired belief each time, each with a different future time and place as examples. Each visualization will reinforce your new belief. Actions which you may have already carried out in the past, and which you can certainly carry out if you wish in the future, can be converted into powerful beliefs. These beliefs will in turn produce more positive actions that will help bring about your outcomes.

Let me remind you that clear visualization is a powerful way to change beliefs and feelings, as well as behaviour. The brain simply does not differentiate between the electrochemical changes resulting from external sensing, and those we create internally—that is, that we imagine. Both, however, become 'experience'. These NLP techniques, therefore, are not just games—they change the very 'landscape' of your brain, and fundamentally affect your life.

New behaviour generator

This is a similar exercise for generating any changes in your own behaviour. You can use it either for generating completely new behaviours, or for making modifications to existing behaviours with which you are not entirely satisfied.

1 First of all, identify the new behaviour you want, or the change that you want in some existing behaviour.

2 Describe to yourself the new behaviour you want, asking yourself, 'How would I look and sound if I were doing that behaviour?'

3 In your imagination, watch yourself producing the behaviour you want in whatever context you want. Other people may be involved in this, in which case you should be aware of their response to your changed behaviour. If you cannot imagine yourself with your new behaviour, then imagine that you are watching some other person doing it, and then put yourself in the place of that person.

4 When you are satisfied with your own performance, step inside yourself in the image and run it through as though you are doing it yourself—that is, become associated. Now, as you go through the motions, pay particular attention to how you feel, as well as to what you see and hear yourself, and also to any response from people around you.

5 If you want to change anything, go back again to step 3, and change your own behaviour, getting back 'into yourself' to check how it feels.

6 When you are happy with your imagined performance and the feelings that accompany it, ask yourself 'What signal will I see, hear or feel, internally or externally, that will let me know when it is time to use this new behaviour?'

7 Finally, imagine that signal happening, use your new behaviour, and then become aware of your feelings of satisfaction.

This new behaviour generator is a useful self-help tool which can assist in personal and professional development. Like any skill, the more you use it, the faster and easier it becomes. The idea is to use it automatically and unconsciously, although, at first, you will probably be self-conscious about the process. Whenever you have an experience that is less than satisfactory, you can process it through your new behaviour generator. Gradually you will take control of your behaviour, and thus the outcomes you achieve.

The swish pattern

The swish is a submodality change pattern that can be used for almost anything, including changing unwanted habits. It is a fast and powerful technique that actually changes the way your brain works.

1 *Identify the context.* First, identify when and where you are stuck, and want to change some well-established habit. Where and when would you like to respond differently to the way you now do?

2 *Identify the first cue picture.* This stage means identifying what you see or experience immediately before you start doing the behaviour that you would like to reject. We have already met this in some of the earlier techniques. When going through this stage, make sure that you are associated—that is, that you see things through your own eyes. Sometimes it may be necessary to carry out the behaviour—that is, induce the actual habit pattern (like taking a chocolate bar from the cupboard)—to become aware of what stimulates it, as we are usually on 'auto-pilot' when we carry out these habits.

3 *Create an outcome picture.* In this stage, you create a picture of how you will see yourself differently if you had *already accomplished* the desired change. At this point, make the picture dissociated; that is, see yourself from somewhere other than through your own eyes (remember how we manipulated submodalities in Chapter 7). Watch this picture and adjust it until it is really attractive.

4 *Swish.* See the first cue picture big and bright. Put a small dark image of the outcome picture in the bottom right-hand corner. Now have the small dark image grow big and bright to cover the first cue picture as it gets dim and shrinks away as fast as you can say swish, then blank out the screen, or open your eyes. Carry out this swish pattern four or five times, taking only a second each and blanking at the end of each one.

5 *Testing.* You can test by a future pace, that we have already met. Picture the first image you imagined and notice what happens. If the

swish pattern has worked, it will be more difficult to get a clear image of your first picture; it will tend to fade or be replaced by the new picture. If not, do a few more swishes and go through the process again.

As well as techniques for controlling how you feel and replacing unwanted limiting beliefs, you now have the ability to change your behaviour. By making changes to the structure of how you think, actual changes in your behaviour will be effective and permanent. You can be as creative as you wish in thinking of ways to apply these principles and techniques personally and professionally.

10 Learning

The principles of goal achievement and communication that we have already met in NLP are ideal models for any learning and training situation. We saw that by fixing a goal, by acting, by observing the results of our behaviour and then, in a flexible way, by changing what we do to bring about the desired goal, we can achieve all manner of success. This feedback loop system, of course, is a classical model for learning. We learn in effect by doing, and especially by making mistakes. And these mistakes are so valuable to the process that we cannot achieve anything worth while without them. NLP does not define them as mistakes, however. As we saw earlier, they are simply information or feedback about a given course of behaviour. You discover what happens when you do or say something, and can try something different if it does not seem to be effective. This is more than a learning model; it is a model for goal achievement.

Many orthodox learning situations do not use this model because of the very nature of what is being taught. Instead of addressing real-life problems, to which we do not know the solution at the outset, much of our learning involves what we might call puzzles, or conundrums. In these cases there is a known answer. The *teacher* knows it, but the students do not. The process, therefore, is one of communicating generations of knowledge from teachers to learners. While this learning process might well involve some activity to reinforce the learning, it does not involve the trial and error of the NLP feedback model—the answer has long since been found by some professor, teacher or trainer. What remains, in orthodox learning of this sort, is to pass on the privileged information or answers in such a way that it will be remembered and regurgitated when needed. The very practical difficulty is that most of our problems do not have a known answer—they are not mere puzzles. Sometimes we do not even know the *question*, although there is no doubt we have a problem. But such rote learning is in any case less effective than learning based on real needs and experience.

In the real world, particularly of business, 'programmed' learning is much too limited. For every puzzle that we face—for which we know there is a solution and it simply remains to find someone who has the answer—there are many more true problems. Even if a similar problem has been met by another organization, it is unlikely that the mix of variables, in particular the individual people involved, will be the same. The NLP model of learning is much closer to the action learning that was popularized by Professor Reg Revans, and is now increasingly used in training and business contexts. In any event, we need a practical *doing* model of learning when acquiring a skill, as distinct from remembering a bit of information or a theory. If, for instance, I want to learn to play bowls, I first need to decide that that is what I *want*, and often an outcome is born below the level of consciousness—we do not always have *written* goals in these situations, but we do need to have a goal. I then 'have a go', and notice where I am not getting it right. I have to be willing to miss the target time and time again, and need the acuity to observe just what is happening that seems to result in different outcomes. With some humility, and the flexibility to change my behaviour, before long I shall be on a steep learning curve as a player of bowls.

My sensory acuity can also be applied to watching others—how they behave and the strategy they seem to use. But I still need to carry out the activity myself to make the learning process work for me. The model applies in any skill involved in training and development. You can read a lot about giving public presentations, for example, from excellent textbooks, but at some stage you need to decide that you want to excel, or at least reach a certain level of competence, in the skill, and you try it. How quickly you will reach a level of competence depends on how accurately you observe what is happening each time you carry out the activity, and also on your level of flexibility to change your behaviour each time you miss the target. The more times you go round this learning loop, and the more times you are willing to make mistakes, the quicker will be the overall learning process. There is not much room for a teacher in this whole process, but a coach, facilitator or encourager can speed up the learning.

Unconscious competence

There is another model of learning that is also very useful. We have already seen that the vast majority of all our behaviours take place at an unconscious level. At some time in the past we have developed a degree of *unconscious competence* in a particular skill, behaviour or activity. But this level of competence was preceded by the trial and error with which we are all familiar in any highly conscious learning situation. Going back to the beginning, we start off in a universal state of *unconscious incompetence* (as regarding a skill, say) or perhaps *unconscious ignorance* (as regarding some area of knowledge). That is, we know neither what we cannot do, nor what we do not know. If you or I pick up a technical journal in a subject well outside our own field of expertise, we shall probably come across not just words and concepts, but whole areas of knowledge that we did not know existed before picking up the journal. Just being *conscious* of the new subject takes us in that instant outside the comfort of unconscious ignorance or unconscious competence, and we now have an awareness of some knowledge or skill. This is the start of any learning—knowledge, skills and all the benefits that follow are now potentially within our reach. We have moved into a new level of learning which we might describe as *conscious incompetence* or *conscious ignorance.* We are ignorant of the subject involved or, incompetent to carry out a behaviour, but now we at least know that we are.

Conscious incompetence is a familiar condition, and applies to the many things that we would like to learn and accomplish. This, of course, is the basis on which all further learning is built. We can never proceed to learn things when we are firmly in the first category of unconscious incompetence; we have not even entered the world of the new learning. And this provides an important lesson in self-development: the more we expose ourselves to new areas of knowledge and behaviour, the more we shall become aware of things that we are now ignorant of, or behaviours that we are incapable of. This may not happen by accident, but is the result of meeting people from different backgrounds, wide reading and general exposure to a world outside our own present limited world. Only by extending this limited world of ours—if you like, our present perceptual map—can we enter into the real world of learning which moves towards the unconscious competence we have observed in excellent people.

The desire to learn something new or acquire a new skill is what then drives us to the next stage. Learning at this stage is a heavily conscious issue, involving many attempts and many failures. Sometimes we find it a struggle, and from time to time want to give up the effort. But in due course we reach a certain level of competence. If we are not falsely modest, most of us can list several areas, covering sports, hobbies, and work, in which we know that we have reached a reasonable level of knowledge and proficiency. This level in the learning process might be described as *conscious competence.*

But still this is not the level of human excellence. As we have seen already, true excellence seems to occur when the person involved is not conscious of what he or she is doing, certainly in any detailed sense. The top golfer, for example, has gone through each of the stages outlined above, before entering the level of unconscious competence— just doing it, without thinking. In most cases, he or she cannot describe fully what is happening when excellent behaviour is being carried out. At this level, the behaviour becomes as automatic as our breathing or pulse rate, or the simplest of day-to-day activities. For this reason the activity can be repeated consistently and without the interference of the critical left brain that tends to reduce our competence in these sort of skills.

The following are the stages in the learning cycle, which leads to unconscious competence and is the foundation of human excellence in so many spheres:

- **unconscious incompetence**
- **conscious incompetence**
- **conscious competence**
- **unconscious competence.**

Like the four-part success model we met in Chapter 2, this learning process forms a continuous loop. We can be highly competent one moment, at a certain level, then become aware of a shortcoming, usually when exposed to someone who is better at the activity. A pianist knows well the feeling walking away from a concert performed by a virtuoso musician, and a sportsperson knows what it means to go back to the drawing board after witnessing a champion perform. But as true competence improves, we again must develop to an unconscious level, which is where real skill lies.

Let us not underestimate the importance of this state of unconscious competence. It is not confined to super sportspeople or geniuses. It is something that we are all very familiar with. If you were to make a list of all your actions on a fairly regular basis throughout your day, many of these will be firmly in the category of unconscious competence. For instance, getting dressed, cleaning your teeth, tying your shoe laces, or driving to work, unconscious of the traffic and immediate environment, are demonstrations of amazing feats of physical co-ordination. The high-speed typing that a secretary does without any fanfare, playing a musical instrument 'by ear', excelling at DIY, or working the video are all examples of unheralded yet unmistakable unconscious competence. The very fact that we tend to down-rate such activities—assuming that everyone else can also do such things easily—is evidence that we have reached the unconscious competence level. We are simply not aware of the amazing complexity of the muscle movements and brain power used in these operations. Imagine a little girl enviously watching her peer successfully tying a shoelace, when clearly she has not been able to do this with all her trying, day after day. And even when she achieves success, for some time she is conscious of her ability. Only with repeated practice does the ability become natural, unaffected, unconscious competence.

We need not even go back to childhood to see examples of the difference that unconscious competence makes. It is difficult to convince a non-swimmer that swimming is as easy as breathing or walking, as of course it is to many natural swimmers. But those natural swimmers have probably long forgotten their early swimming attempts, which produced many failures. The behaviour of swimming, like tying shoelaces or getting dressed, has been relegated to unconscious competence. There is no longer the awareness of either carrying out the activity or of just how clever the action is.

A popular example of how this learning model works is in learning to drive a car. When we start off there is plenty of conscious incompetence. We know very well what we cannot do and find it most frustrating. Hardly anything seems to come naturally, and it seems impossible (in fact it is) to think about so many things at the same time. All drivers then reach the point—and ironically, this can sometimes be long after passing a driving test—where they have driven from A to B without realizing they have actually done the journey. In other words, they have become *natural* drivers, reaching a level (at least in the basic skill of driving) of unconscious competence. As long as the behaviour carries on (that is, there is practice), the basic competence continues to be automatic, or unconscious. Exposure to a better driver, or reading an article about advanced driving, however, might bring, once again, an awareness of incompetence. And the quest for improvement continues—the cycle starts again.

There is no limit, it seems, to the level of competence that can be achieved 'without thinking'. The late Ayrton Senna, the Formula One racing driver, talked of being one with his car, and described a race in almost spiritual terms. With all the driving processes carried out automatically, the conscious mind can, of course, concentrate on tactics, or the unique aspects of the race, which is where an important edge can be gained. This is the partnership of right and left brain that characterizes excellence in any sphere.

11 Language and the Meta Model

Words and language are an essential part of our thinking, and are associated with left-brain processing. This is where conscious thought happens, and much conscious thought is based on language—for instance when we ask ourselves 'What if . . .'. So-called verbal reasoning and classical logic relies on language as its raw material for high-level thinking. Although true creativity sometimes seems to transcend verbal reasoning—at least until reason catches up with insight—the language we use can be very helpful in stimulating more creative, lateral thought. The reframing techniques in Chapter 6 were examples of language patterns used to harness more creative, quality thinking, and opening up choices through new perspectives. The Meta Model is another powerful NLP model concerned with language and the way we use words. It is another way to reframe, is a powerful tool in communication, and is important enough to justify an entire chapter. As a single model, it can transform the way you think, and add professionalism to your T&D role.

We cannot, of course, separate words from thinking, and in seeking to understand mental maps, the words that we use give lots of clues as to our perceptions. The Meta Model first divides language between what is termed surface structure and deep structure. An example of language at the surface structure might be 'a cake was made'. At a deep structure level the statement might be, 'Jane made a delicious cake in less than ten minutes'. Then what is termed reference structure translates the language into sensory experience, that is, visual, auditory and kinaesthetic terms. The Meta Model then identifies three main ways in which our individual models of reality fall short of reality.

1 *Deletions.* In much of what we say we *omit* information. Communication would become quite unbearable, in fact, if we transferred to the other person all the details in our mind. Therefore, whether by design or default, large chunks of information are omitted as a matter of course.
2 *Distortions.* We frequently distort our experience of sensory data, and this is reflected also in the language we use.
3 *Generalizations.* Much of what we say is generalized. For instance, the

assumptions we all make and beliefs we hold are likely to form generalizations.

The Meta Model identifies various patterns of language in which deletions, distortions and generalizations appear. By being able to recognize these, you will be in a strong position to question and get a better understanding about any communication. It helps us to understand the other person's map of reality.

Deletions

Deletions comprise several types of language pattern, each with its own NLP description. Some of the descriptions sound very technical, but the language patterns themselves are common, and you are likely to meet them scores of times throughout the day. You may want to make up your own descriptions to make them easier to remember.

Nominalizations   You might hear the expression: 'I just want appreciation.' 'Appreciation', of course, is just a word or name—a nominalization. To get more meaning from the statement, the question that might follow is: 'How do you want to be appreciated?' Nominalizations often turn verbs (like appreciate) into nouns (like appreciation), thus eliminating the whole process of action. By asking the question, 'Just how do you want to be appreciated?', we elicit more meaning from what otherwise can be an abstract word. A nominalization is not a tangible or concrete thing, so a good test is: 'Can I wrap this in a parcel?' If not, it is probably a nominalization. By getting back from the abstraction to the process or action, you can get a much better understanding of what is happening. A trainer who uses a lot of nominalizations usually comes across as boring or unintelligible, and the same applies to a written report. These words do not usually fire the imagination.

Unspecified verbs   Some verbs leave a lot of information unsaid. For instance, you might hear the expression, 'He let me down.' The sort of question the Meta Model would suggest is: 'How exactly did he let you down?' The information missing from the way the verb is used is often crucial to the real meaning. Sometimes there is a purpose in being vague, and the purpose, or outcome, will always determine the language to be used in a communication. Similarly, surface level language, which we use in everyday communication and which is on the whole very efficient, does not provide deeper meaning—sometimes you have to ask for it. The important thing, by recognizing these recurring information language patterns, is to spot a deletion when you meet one.

Unspecified nouns   A noun can have lots of meanings depending on how a person uses the word. For instance, someone might say: 'I need a break.' The question that can then be posed is: 'What sort of a break?' or 'A break from what?' The noun as it is used is unspecified, and does not tell us much.

Simple deletions   In this case, information is simply missing or deleted from a statement. For instance, you might hear the expression: 'She is annoyed.' The question you can ask in this case is: 'Annoyed about what, or whom?' You simply need more information.

Comparative deletions   Another variety of deletions is where some standard of comparison is not given. You might hear the comment, for instance: 'He is a better speaker.' The question that has to be raised is: 'Better than whom?' Whenever comparisons are being made you can elicit more understanding by asking about the standards or comparisons being used.

Lack of referential index   Forgive the NLP terminology, but in this case a pronoun is used and we do not know who the pronoun refers to. For instance, someone might say, 'They never do anything.' The question to ask is: 'Who are *they*? Who, specifically, do not do anything or never do anything?'

These six illustrations of missing information in everyday language patterns show just how little real understanding is transmitted in normal communication. But they also illustrate how simple it is to gain the missing information, and clarify understanding. These patterns often overlap—a single statement might include several deletions.

Distortions

Certain language patterns indicate distortions of meaning. The Meta Model gives five examples.

Presuppositions   Often what we say *presupposes* some truth which is not necessarily valid. For instance, someone might say: 'I can't study at my age.' The question that can be put is: 'In what way is your age preventing you from studying?' For the statement to make sense, the presupposition that age is a factor in our ability to study would have to be true. The Meta Model line of questioning seeks to identify and question the validity of any presupposition.

Mind reading   This is a familiar form of language of which we are all guilty, where someone seems to assume knowledge of how another person thinks, or that person's internal state of mind. For instance, someone might say to you: 'You don't trust me.' This can well be termed mind reading, and the question that needs to be asked is: 'How do you know I don't trust you?' or 'What exactly leads you to believe that?'

Cause and effect   This pattern involves the old question of whether there is a link between cause and apparent effect. Let us say that someone makes the statement: 'Her manner makes me nervous.' The question then should be: 'How does her manner make you nervous?' or, more specifically, 'How do you make yourself nervous by her manner?' In this case the cause and effect distortion implies that one person's action has caused another person's emotional reaction. There may well be a causal link, but more often than not this language device is used (unwittingly of course) as a convenient reason to apportion blame, and unload personal responsibility. To expose this distortion, question the link between an apparent cause and an apparent effect. Put the onus on the speaker who alone has charge of his or her personal emotions. The environment of a participative training seminar is usually replete with this and other examples of Meta Model.

Complex equivalents   Frequently we link two experiences and interpret them as being synonymous. Our understanding, in effect, is that X means Y. For example, you might hear the expression: 'He's always interfering, he doesn't trust me.' The question to pose here is: 'How does his interfering mean that he doesn't trust you?' Usually the link is in the mind—that is, the perceptual map of the speaker—and has no rational basis.

Lost performative   In this language pattern, value judgements or rules and opinions are assumed to have validity, but the source of these values is not given. For instance, imagine the expression: 'It's bad mannered to be late (or early).' The response here might be: 'How do you know it is bad mannered to be late?' or, perhaps, 'Who says so?' The Meta Model response seeks the source of the value judgement that has influenced the statement.

Generalizations

The third category of Meta Model language patterns is generalizations. These patterns are heard all around us every day, and illustrate the speaker's limited model of the world.

Universal quantifiers   This one is easy to recognize because certain words keep recurring such as *all, no one, always, never* or *every*. For example, you might hear the expression: 'She never joins in anything.' The response would be to form a question of the universal word *never*, asking quite simply: 'Never?' or you can add: 'Was there *ever* a time that she joined in?' These universal quantifiers are very much part of our language and our everyday conversation is full of them. Invariably, the response question reveals the inaccuracy or absurdity of the universal quantifier and opens up another perspective on the situation that can help understanding and communication. Often a so-called problem is only a problem because it is couched in these absolute terms—there is no room for manoeuvre, no hope, no choice. Therefore, common little words take on unreasonable power if they are not spotted quickly and treated for what they are worth. Fortunately, this pattern is easy to spot once you are aware of it.

Modal operator of possibility   This language pattern concerns what we think we can or cannot do. The words to watch out for are those that imply that we have no choice. They are easy to spot in everyday conversation, often incorporating negative words like *can't*, *haven't* or *won't*. An example of a phrase might be: 'I can't handle it on my own.' A response might be: 'What would happen if you did?' or 'What stops you from handling it on your own?'

Modal operator of necessity   This is a similar pattern, but in this case the words that we are particularly interested in are those that seem to imply necessity, such as *must, must not, have to, should* and *shouldn't*, or the phrase *it is necessary*. For example, you might hear the expression: 'I have to be there very early.' The response might be: 'What would happen if you were not?' The response asks whether a particular action is necessary. Watch out for either positive words like *ought*, or negative words like *ought not*, that seem to indicate necessity. Such language is very common and reveals the many values and beliefs we each hold that go unquestioned, yet limit both communication and achievement.

In each of these cases we sought to make a generalization more specific, which gives us both understanding and choices.

It is important to say, at this point, that the way we handle questions or responses to Meta Model patterns is very important. Our intention, of course, is to improve communication and aid understanding—to mutually enrich respective maps of the world. We should avoid causing bad feeling or animosity, so in everyday conversation be very sparing in your use of questioning, and always seek to gain the maximum rapport in anything you say or do. A useful exercise, however, is to mentally respond to the various Meta Model statements rather than speak them out. This will tend to change your own perspective on the communication, opening up a different understanding, and possibly change your state of mind. Some phrases are used without much thought for the feelings of the person being addressed, yet can be packed with emotional force, especially in the case of the universal quantifier *always* or *never*, and rarely justify strong feelings. A 'reversed' response 'Always?' or 'Never?', however, can be just as emotionally received. So, initially the Meta Model can help in controlling your own state, then extended both to gaining further understanding about a communication and on to changing also the state of the speaker. So rapport remains the crucial factor in this or any other communication, and the way in which a response is made will make the net effect constructive or damaging.

The Meta Model helps us to recognize the enormous variety of perceptual maps in the people with whom we communicate. Each one of these examples of deletions, distortions and generalizations indicates both the uniqueness of our individual way of thinking, and also the severe limitations we place on ourselves when we are restricted to a narrow map of the world. Even a simple awareness of the model and what the patterns indicate can give immediate benefit. Because we are aware of the way language is misused, it is less likely that we shall react emotionally, or misinterpret a communication. We can be almost certain that the words or phrases used are surface level, and that there is deeper meaning behind the statement.

Using the Metal Model

The Meta Model can be used in many ways. Having spotted a pattern, you might choose not to react in any overt way at all to a statement made, however preposterous it might seem. Simply recognizing the pattern will affect how you feel about the communication. You will no doubt be more objective and dispassionate—more in control—so you can gain benefit yourself without speaking a word.

Alternatively, by carefully and sensitively questioning the communicator, you can elicit more understanding of the true meaning the speaker intends to convey. In this way you can act as an agent or catalyst to help the other person clarify his or her meaning, while gaining rapport. You will no doubt help to further your own goals in the process.

There are lots of different language patterns to recognize and remember, so it might take some time before the Meta Model becomes an instinctive skill that you can use in everyday life. I suggest that you start with one or two patterns, such as the universal quantifiers which involve words that are very easy to spot, and then move on to extend your skills to other parts of the model.

One way to gain experience in the use of the model is to work through a piece of written prose, such as a newspaper article, and try to spot as many different Meta Model patterns as you can. Initially you may have difficulty putting a name to the patterns, but it should not be long before you can at least recognize them—for instance, 'mind reading' and 'cause and effect'. You might start to spot 'comparative deletions' from give-away words such as better or worse. When doing the exercise from a book or newspaper article, watch out for cases where more than one pattern is incorporated in the same phrase or sentence. For instance, the phrase 'You never know how I feel' is both an example of a distortion, 'mind reading', and also a generalization, the 'universal quantifier' *never*.

You will gain further practice by simply listening to conversation in your normal work or socially. It is surprising how many of these patterns you will hear in 15 to 20 minutes in a committee meeting or group discussion, or even in one-to-one conversation with a colleague. Once you are familiar with the way these patterns repeat themselves, and are able to prepare a few standard responses—questions or comments that might elicit a better understanding of what is being said—you can start to practise in real life. The rule is to always maintain or achieve better rapport with the person with whom you are communicating.

Applications in training

This is an ideal tool for what we term 'thinking on your feet', in any training or public-speaking context. Because so much of our language contains these deletions, distortions and generalizations, you will have a standard pattern of response that will certainly seem instinctive to those around. You will be seen, for instance, to be incisive in getting to the core of what is being said, or perceptive, and probably a good listener. Furthermore, during any verbal exchange and clarification you will have a good opportunity to consider the content or any technical aspects of a question or comment—you will 'buy time'. This is a very professional approach to thinking on your feet, and will become a skill in time. It enables you to get nearer to reality in any communication by probing the individual maps of others. It also helps you to maintain emotional control in dialogue with individuals who might otherwise have annoyed you. You keep control.

Training and other professionals are, of course, as likely to use defective language patterns as any one else. One effect of filling our language with these patterns is that a speech or training presentation can become uninteresting, and the communication is thus ineffective. This is because so many of our words may be abstract in nature, nominalizations and generalizations, and not easily visualized—a good test of clear communication. By being aware of our own language limitations we can add richness to what we say, and thus improve the calibre of our communication. If the constant use of inefficient language patterns by others causes us annoyance, or even anger from time to time, it is reasonable to expect that we may have the same effect on others, even if they are not aware of exactly what is wrong with what is being said in a language sense. So much offence is caused and emotion aroused by the loose use of universal quantifiers, for example, that the well-earned rapport of the most positive trainee can be easily lost.

You can therefore make a big improvement in your training and public speaking performance by making a start on your own use of these language patterns. You need to be very familiar with the whole model, and gradually eliminate the different categories of deficiency from your own communication. This will give you a clearer and richer personal map, but it will also create a better rapport with those with whom you are in contact. Practise the model in quite small doses, until it gradually becomes instinctive. Whenever you are *conscious* about doing something you will not do it very well, and you can quickly ruin an important presentation or seminar by thinking too much (at the time, that is) about what you are doing. This applies to almost any activity, and specially one where you are in the public view, so start off by recognizing the Meta Model patterns in others, both in spoken language and in writing, such as memos, reports and books, without making any 'response'. When you are familiar with the patterns, start noticing them in your own language, and even in your self-talk if it is negative ('You will never manage that', 'You can't handle that'). Using the model personally, your responses will, of course, be mental. Using the technique in a group or one-to-one situation, you can begin to make some important changes to your communication and see improvements in mutual understanding.

NLP has rightly recognized the importance of words and language in all our communication. Recent research has shown that words can be just as powerful as prescription drugs in changing our behaviour. In his work at UCLA, psychiatrist Dr Lewis Baxter has proved that carefully chosen words can activate the same areas of the brain as a highly prescribed drug, so the therapeutic value of language has been established. Words can indeed heal, and we all know from experience how they can have a strong effect on our emotions. A few well-chosen words can have a major effect on students or learners in all kinds of situations. In the past you may have 'chosen your words' as a matter of courtesy. You now have more choices, and the technology in the form of this language-based model to improve your communication and change your behaviour.

The Meta Model as a problem-solving tool

The Meta Model is primarily used in communication, allowing us to enrich our own perceptual maps of reality, and to open windows on others. In combination with some of the other reframing techniques we have met, this model can also be used as an important problem-solving tool. Some of the statements which indicate distortions of language represent the very problems—often people problems—that we meet in our day-to-day work. 'He never listens' or 'She's better than me', while probably faulty in their literal truth, nevertheless constitute real problems for the speaker. The Meta Model responses are no more than devices to reframe a particular statement, or the problem it represents. The model can be applied to business as well as personal problems.

You might hear the remark: 'His department is poorly organized.' There are several possible Meta Model patterns implicit in this single statement. It might imply, for example, that the whole of the department, and all the work, is poorly organized. Some comparison is also implicit, presumably with better organized departments in the company or outside. You can therefore address this as a problem-statement and ask such questions as: 'By what comparison?', 'Who says so?', 'Is *all* of the department poorly organized, or is there some aspect of the work that needs putting right?', and finally, 'How, *specifically*, is his department poorly organized?' Each question, which can be easily constructed based on the standard Metal Model responses, will reframe the situation and probably help you to identify the problem in a better way. At the very worst, it will open up new perspectives on what initially seems to be the problem. It might suggest a more specific problem that can be readily acted upon, or, it may make the 'problem' all but disappear.

Problems that relate to people, and involve a lot of subjectivity and feeling, are quite amenable to the Meta Model as a problem-solving tool, in the same way that we used the other language-based Points of View technique. In this case, we are not necessarily using the Meta Model in ordinary day-to-day conversation, but to identify problems, which are clarified and quantified by the responses.

12 Strategies for success

So far, you have drawn mainly on your own past experiences. But in NLP you are not restricted to yourself as a model. You can imagine what another person might see, hear and feel in a given situation, and thus change how you feel by 'getting into their shoes'. It helps, of course, if you can first observe the person you wish to model at fairly close hand, paying particular attention to his or her movements and body language. We saw earlier how physical movements affect how we think, and modelling someone else physically will assist us to assume his or her state of mind. If the 'successful' person walks in a confident upright manner, maybe a little faster than you walk, then model yourself on his or her physiology—if you want to achieve what that person achieves. Notice how it feels to move and behave as that person does.

You can go a lot further in modelling other people. You can *elicit* from them their mental strategy—by asking them. To do this you need to determine the visual, auditory and kinaesthetic modalities that they experience based on their description of a particular event or behaviour, then the many submodalities of those representation systems. Therefore, you do not just depend on observing and copying physical behaviour, but can also 'borrow' someone else's thought submodalities in your own thinking when in a particular situation. In this way you will not only *act* like the model, but you will *think* like the model, identifying and using the model's 'thinking strategy'.

NLP has given us a major advantage over earlier positive thinking techniques. We now have a better language in which to communicate thoughts, and a model to understand states of mind. Recalling the presupposition 'the map is not the territory' we can now begin to understand the process of each other's perceptual maps. The content of thought is not important for our personal purposes—what makes one person happy makes another person sad, and what motivates one person bores another. But understanding the thought process or strategy—the combination of unique submodalities which go together to make the empowering thoughts—can bring dramatic benefits. Successful strategies do not depend on the 'content' of thought, so you do not have to wait for events and circumstances to happen before you can have the state of mind you want. A person can be highly motivated, or content in the midst of the same external 'reality' as would make another person depressed, bored or angry. Rather, the characteristics of those thought patterns and their structure determine whether a strategy is empowering or disempowering, and the accompanying state of mind.

When you know what to look for there is a greater chance of finding it. You now know what to look for in modelling excellence—the behaviour patterns and the thinking patterns of the excellent person. That first presupposition now has even more potency. As well as appreciating the other person's map, his or her own perspective on the world, you now have some technology to 'read' that map. The other person, in turn, can have a glimpse into your map of reality. Thus we can compare each other's perceptual maps of the world around us. We can recognize a richer map when we see one. One person, for instance, may be confident in an area in which you are anxious, and you can draw on that person's thought processes to help you in that situation. You might have a particular appreciation of music or art, or have acquired a particular instinctive skill, so you, in turn, can share the thought patterns that are associated with these aspects of your personal map. Winning 'strategies' can be elicited and used to advantage to bring about similar success.

You will have realized by now what a large part our ability to visualize plays in NLP. It is not sufficient to have a theoretical knowledge of a model of thought processes and the language of modalities and submodalities. We need the skill to recognize, use and manipulate our own thought processes for our advantage. Like any physical skill this takes time and practice before you become proficient. At first it might seem difficult to differentiate between, for instance, the many subtle auditory characteristics of different memories or forthcoming activities. However, with practice and some perseverance, you will get to know yourself—that is, your real self, and the way you think—in a far deeper way. You will then recognize subtle differences in the way you think which, in turn, accounts for the subtle difference of your state of mind from time to time. This increased skill in personal thought manipulation will pay enormous dividends when you begin to apply the principles and techniques of NLP to achieve your specific outcomes. All our thinking strategies, which we use unconsciously, either empower us or disempower us in achieving those outcomes.

Success characteristics

Some characteristics seem to accompany success in almost any field. These are quite standard and reappear from time to time in all sorts of books dealing with success and positive thinking. These are essentially mental strategies—ways of thinking, attitudes and beliefs. Such strategies can now be modelled, and form the basis of personal mastery in any skill. I shall identify some of these, and relate them to the principles of NLP. We can then differentiate between simple positive thinking and the science of communication and goal achievement.

Passion   This is an old-fashioned term, but even a cursory look through history will indicate that achievers had a remarkable passion for what they were doing. Their goals were supported by feelings and emotions. Frequently we attribute personal discipline or willpower to success, but what drives one person to get up earlier than another in the morning, or to go that extra mile in commitment, is the passion held for his or her outcome. Both heart and mind are involved. Empowering passion is a state of mind that can be induced, and most of us are passionate about something. NLP allows us to transfer passion—or any other useful state of mind—to another activity or situation for our benefit as we saw in Chapter 7. This 'passion strategy' has to be identified in the language of thought processes—representation systems or modalities, and their submodalities, in the way we have already described. You can even have an anchor which arouses passion on demand if you use the resources anchoring technique I also covered in Chapter 7. The importance of this characteristic underlies the importance of your state of mind—how you feel about something—and its effect on your behaviour. It can be more important than even technical knowledge and experience.

Belief   As we have seen, our beliefs about what we *are* and what we *can* be determine almost wholly what we shall be. To a very large extent, what we believe will come to pass, especially if this concerns ourselves (self-beliefs) and relates to outcomes within our sphere of control—hence the importance of 'well-formed outcomes'. If you believe that you are limited in all sorts of ways, either because of your environment, education or level of talent, then in a quite amazing way your belief will be self-fulfilling. We restrict ourselves to the boundaries of our beliefs. Those individuals who seem to achieve most have much wider belief boundaries, although in other respects they may not seem so special. Sometimes their beliefs seem to go beyond what is reasonable and logical, yet nevertheless they bring about outstanding achievements. Countless anecdotes confirm that so-called impossible dreams become possible time and time again. Like passion, beliefs are represented by different ways of perceiving, different mental strategies which can either be useful or hold us back.

Perhaps the most debilitating belief is that we are *stuck with* those beliefs that have hitherto resulted in our limitations. This is where NLP can help, as we saw in Chapter 8. Beliefs can be changed in a quite specific way. When might you want to believe something different? In some situations we can be angry and incensed about something but do not *believe* we have the ability to do anything about it. It is possible to have passionate feelings about something and yet still have limiting beliefs. But when you link passion with a strong belief in yourself and what you are capable of, you have a recipe for goal achievement. With NLP, belief, as well as feelings, are negotiable. You do not have to believe what you do not want to believe. But you can change a disempowering belief if you want to. The behaviour changing techniques covered in Chapter 9 can be used to advantage.

Strategy   But it does not stop there. We need to organize ourselves and our resources in a sensible way that will bring about what we are trying to achieve. In a corporate situation, we shall not get far without an understandable, coherent strategy of how we intend to get where we want to be. And, as we saw earlier, this is also fundamental to personal achievement. Besides acting as a blueprint, or plan of action, because it is logically and rationally stated, a clear strategy can also be communicated. You can thus pass on to others your own map of success.

From a cognitive point of view, we have strategies for almost everything we do. A strategy for spelling, a strategy for mental arithmetic, a strategy for tying our shoelaces, a strategy for getting out of bed in the morning. In most cases these strategies, although well established as thought patterns, operate below the level of consciousness—they are thinking habits—so you may need to determine your own strategy in a particular activity to better understand what it is that makes you succeed in one area and fail in another. Similarly, by being able to elicit the strategy of another person through the language of NLP, you can also learn successful strategies from others. This ability to observe, identify and understand the strategies of others is a major source of personal excellence, and forms the foundation of the very idea of modelling success. We have already seen that in a training and development context we are all too lacking when it comes to defining very clear goals and objectives. Another weakness might be in defining a clear strategy for achieving those objectives. To succeed, both personally and in a business situation, our passion and beliefs need to be harnessed into a workable strategy.

Values   One of the biggest factors that emerged during my research with top business leaders was the importance of personal values. Each leader, and his or her organization, is affected by a different vision, and different strategies have been designed to reach these visions. But underpinning these visions and strategies are the values of both the leader and the people in the organization which form the vital culture upon which any success is based. It is significant that relatively few key values, such as integrity and respect for the individual person, seemed to underpin successful people and businesses. Values are, of course, very closely linked to our belief systems, and, like fundamental beliefs, tend to have their origins early in life. When doing the ecology check that was part of the goal clarification exercise in Chapter 3, one of the factors that frequently arose was that of values. Everything about a goal or objective can be ideal until you sense that it conflicts with some deep value—a value that is not well articulated but nevertheless affects your motivation and how you 'feel' about something. Once you achieve congruence between your objectives and your values, you increase the chance of success many times.

Energy

Somehow the passion we met earlier is converted into extraordinary energy, and this too was a factor that was seen in top leadership. In some cases it could be seen in a very physical way in the sense that some people seem to drive themselves to work long hours in a way that others would find impossible. But then it transpires that it is the *goal* or purpose which creates this energy. The same person, without a driving goal and some passion about what is to be done, has no more energy, it seems, than the next person. Success is not divided into intellectual success and physical success. All our powers, mental, physical and spiritual, seem to be combined in an energy that converts the very best of whatever resources we have into action and results. Experienced trainers are familiar with how the energy level of a group can be transformed when they have a motivating task to achieve.

Rapport

NLP has been called the science of communication, and this is an area where many recent developments have been made. As we saw in Chapter 5, the major factor in successful communication is the rapport that is created between people. When people are on the same wavelength, formal communication hardly seems necessary. NLP has shown us the basis of this rapport, and how it can be established. We know, for instance, that our sensory preference—that is, a preference to think in pictures, sounds or feelings—is a major factor in whether we can work with someone or not. And this can easily be identified using the various cues we discussed. Achieving outcomes, particularly in business, usually involves people, and when people are involved the critical factor is rapport. This is also the case in leadership, in that no leader can succeed for long without a following of people. He or she needs to establish rapport at every level. Many of the leaders I met were towards the introvert end of the personality scale, and yet had the wisdom and skill to be able to build up rapport with the key people around them. A large number of those around us who we would classify as successful have come to master communication. They have learned not just the importance of people in bringing about their goals, but how rapport can be established. Just 'liking' a teacher at school has influenced learning in particular subjects and the consequent careers and lives of millions. And the effect of rapport is no less in the case of adults in a training context. Establishing rapport is the first objective for a trainer.

Modelling NLP had its origins in the practice of modelling excellent behaviour, but modelling has always been seen as a major factor in success from the earliest of positive thinking writers. The theories and techniques of management science and training and development have given little place for modelling, however, over the decades. But most of us instinctively know the importance of modelling our behaviour on another person or persons. Top achievers in business, sport and politics invariably cite personal models they have sought to emulate. Usually we can look back to a friend, boss or work colleague, or some well-known personality who had a major influence on our lives. However, although forming an important part of our own later achievement, this modelling process was probably a hit-and-miss affair, of which we were unaware at the time. By understanding the principles involved, including the thought patterns on which successful people operate, we are now in a position to model others in a more scientific way.

Mental strategies These characteristics of success, although widely accepted, have usually been interpreted very subjectively and sometimes surrounded with the mystique which we often attribute to outstandingly successful people. But, based on the idea of unconscious competence, which accounts for these outstanding skills and achievements, such mental strategies are within the reach of all of us. In fact, as we saw when discussing this aspect of learning and excellence in Chapter 10, each of us exhibits unconscious competence in one or more areas. And we are aware of the feeling of mastery and flow that accounts for our own successes. NLP takes the mystique out of this. We have had no difficulty in accepting that people of similar physical stature and fitness can achieve a level of competence when measured in physical terms. But we now know that our minds—at least the hardware—is just as standard, and that we can programme the way we think just as we can get physically fit by practising physical strategies. We have a language of representation systems and modalities that can be used both to get the best out of what we already are, and to bridge the gap to other people's mental strategies. At the level of mastery it is the mental aspects of behaviour that seem to be the most significant—that is where control of what seem like external behaviour and skills take place.

The ingredients of excellence

NLP makes its own contribution to 'success criteria', identifying three fundamental ingredients that must apply if we are to reproduce human excellence. Not surprisingly, these overlap with the general success characteristics I have already discussed. The first is a person's **belief** system. We know the power of belief in bringing about attitudes, feelings and behaviours, and by identifying the belief system in successful people we have a major pointer towards his or her success. Having identified a belief system that is empowering, the hurdle that remains is whether you or I can believe what the other person believes and so bring about the kind of behaviours that produce his or her success. Therefore, as well as identifying beliefs as important, as we saw in Chapter 8, NLP provides techniques to change those that are limiting. And we make changes out of choice, deciding that a particular disempowering belief is no longer worth keeping, and that in its place we want a belief that will help us to bring about our goals.

Second, we must get to know a person's mental **syntax** or strategy for organizing his or her thoughts. This is like a code system guaranteeing success. We may have all the digits of a person's telephone number, but only if we get them in the correct order can we reach the right destination. It is just like baking a cake—there is order or syntax to what you do, and this is usually what makes the important difference. The same is true in any communication. It is not just what we do or say, but how we do things and say things, and the order in which it all happens. When we talk of individual perceptual maps, we mean that each person has a whole range of mental strategies or syntax that determine all his or her behaviours and achievements. NLP enables us to identify the internal strategy underpinning any successful behaviour.

The third ingredient of success we can observe in excellent people is their **physiology**. We know, of course, that the mind and the body are totally linked, and the way that we use our bodies—the way we breathe, our posture, facial expressions and all our movements—can actually influence our state of mind. We saw the power of physiology in the mirroring and the pacing and leading techniques we covered in Chapter 5. Conversely, we know that our state of mind tends to determine our behaviour and, in turn, what we achieve. Therefore, we need to look at physiology, along with the less visible belief systems and mental syntax of any person that we model. In fact we are modelling physiology all the time and have been doing so since childhood. The way that we match body language without thinking, to bring about rapport, is an example of physiological modelling.

Combining these three ingredients, we have three readily open doors to all manner of success. It remains simply to locate those models of excellence on which we want to base our own performance, and elicit from them the necessary strategies and beliefs. Fortunately, NLP has established that certain mental strategies and beliefs tend to empower us more or less universally. We know, for example, that certain strategies for reading and learning can be readily emulated by anyone who wishes to improve his or her own standards. Similarly, and quite obviously, a belief system that says 'I can' is more empowering than one that says 'I cannot'. And an outcome that is imagined clearly, in a focused lifelike way, is more likely to happen than a fuzzy wish. Therefore, we can draw on universal, standard winning strategies. But you can also draw on your own rich personal experience, including the state of mastery as we shall see below, as well as on specific success models you choose. Once you are familiar with the principles and techniques of NLP, you have the opportunity to improve dramatically your performance and goal hit-rate in the areas you choose.

Accessing your mastery state of mind

However you rate yourself as successful or unsuccessful, you can probably think back to an occasion when you had *mastery* of an activity or situation. You experienced at the time a 'mastery state of mind', and NLP can help you to access this mastery state when you want to. Any successful experience can be recalled, amplified or amended, and used in the future whenever you need to call on such an empowering state of mind. As we have seen, our memories are stored in pictures and sounds just like a television screen, and the other sensory modalities with which we have become familiar. You can use these stored memories to improve your future states and thus performance in all sorts of areas. This is a good strategy to access as it represents true excellence, yet is transferable from one area to another. You can capitalize on your own mastery in any personal or social field and benefit your work and professional life, or vice versa. The following steps show how you can access and use your mastery state of mind. You are already familiar with the processes of recalling and future pacing; all you have to do, therefore, is apply the mastery state.

1 Think back to a specific time and place you acted with mastery, either at work, in a sport, perhaps, or in some social or domestic capacity.
2 Relive the experience, taking all the time you need to appreciate how you felt, as well as what happened. See, hear and feel the experience all over again. Notice all the submodalities that were described in Chapter 4 (Table 4.1) and make a note of these.
3 Clear your mind (for instance, by spelling your name backwards).
4 Select some area in your life in which you have a certain level of competence, but in which you feel you have not yet achieved mastery. Choose an activity or experience that you are able, vividly, to see, hear and feel.
5 Step into that experience and notice all the submodalities, then come out of the experience.
6 Notice which submodalities differ as between the two experiences— the one in which you are merely competent and the one in which you experienced true mastery.
7 Clear your mind (for instance, divide your age by four to arrive at a remainder).
8 Once again think of the experience you have just recalled, in which you have not yet experienced a state of mastery, and this time transform it into the mastery state of mind by simply switching a mastery submodality to replace the one that applied in your visualization.
9 Notice how this action of switching submodalities changes your

feelings and perceptions. Take your time to fully appreciate your new changed state. Enjoy the clarity of mind and the feeling of confidence this brings.

Think of situations in which you can use your mastery state of mind. As you mentally rehearse these, and apply empowering submodalities, you will be able to feel the mastery state you have experienced previously. If you are unsure about identifying submodalities, look back to Chapter 4. If you want to be able to call on your mastery state at short notice, refresh you mind by re-reading the anchoring technique in Chapter 7.

Life contents

We have seen how we differ in terms of our personal sensory preference, and we know from the idea of different perceptual maps how each of us sees his or her own world in different ways. NLP has identified some other main differences in the way that we experience the content of our lives. Like sensory preferences, these are ways of perceiving that are quite long-standing—they tend to stay with us over a long period of our lives. However, there can be great value in getting to know these life content characteristics both of our own lives and the lives of others. Unlike strategies used for a specific skill or behaviour, these strategies operate at a higher level, and are deeply ingrained as thinking habits. They represent the macro level of our personal strategies for behaviour. This model identifies five distinct ways of experiencing: doing, knowing, getting/having, relating and being. First we shall see how these five tendencies appear in each of us.

Doing   Are you action orientated? Do you prefer to *do* things before getting to know a lot about them? Do you frequently use words like doing, action, moving, building and so on? Are you the sort of person who will tend to ask: 'What needs to be done around here?' Most models of personality and learning style identify this particular characteristic of action.

Knowing With some people it is important to *understand* or *know* something, and typically they will learn all there is to learn about a new activity, skill or behaviour before they venture into doing anything. In some cases, the knowledge or understanding seem to be the end product—the outcome itself—and people are satisfied with knowing without actually experiencing the thing in real life. They value knowledge for its own sake. Such people tend to buy lots of books and often use the words 'know', 'understand', 'study', 'learn', 'find out' and so on. If you are such a person, you will probably read all the literature you can find about a car or new computer before you commit yourself to buying.

Getting/having   There is another category of people who are primarily interested in things. They need to *get* and to *have* for their main satisfaction. They are acquisitive, wanting to get more of the world round about them, and use words like 'getting', 'having', 'things', 'acquiring' and 'mine'. This is not always in terms of material possessions or the evidence of wealth and outward success. Sometimes, for instance, a person wants evidence of some achievement such as learning a language or acquiring a skill in the form of a certificate or other tangible recognition. Although what we *get* might be of itself worthless, and just symbolic of some activity or achievement, it is important to *have* something physical, a *thing* that will illustrate either what we know or what we have done. People who concentrate on getting and having are likely to put knowing and understanding in second place. They would tend to buy the car or hi-fi, enjoying the pleasure of having, and read the manuals in due course, if ever.

Relating   *Relating* to others is another important category in terms of what is important in the overall content of our lives. Are you a people person? Do you care more about how people feel than what they are doing or what they have learned? Do you use words like 'relating', 'communication', or 'feeling' ? A person to whom relating is important will tend to put *what people think* high on their agenda. For instance, the kind of club you attend, or car you buy, or sports you get involved in, will be with an eye to what someone thinks—perhaps family, friends or colleagues or some respected role model.

Being   Finally, is *place* more important to you? Are you interested in *where*, both physically and in a metaphorical sense? Do you use words like 'place', 'home' and 'being'? Some people use the term 'I want to be' rather than 'I want to know', or to do, or to get or to have. This is strongly associated with personal identity, who and where you are in the world, or some other context. One person might say 'I am a writer' (being), while another might say 'I write books' (doing).

Each of these ways of experiencing the content of our lives will determine our behaviour in given situations. If you are not already familiar with the one that is predominant in your own life, think back to different occasions, such as major purchases or holidays, or pastimes and social involvement to see whether any way seems to come first. Most people who are action-oriented know this because they always seem to get involved in things before the other person. They do not need a second chance when called to the front of a training seminar or, when given the opportunity to carry out even some daring activity. They often love travel because of the new experiences it opens up: they want to get out and do things for themselves. The knowing person, on the other hand, is more inclined to get all the information possible before making a commitment to do anything, and often gets no further than the knowing part of the process. Getting and having are easy to recognize in people who are always acquiring the latest gadget, or all the visible paraphernalia of a modern home and business. But there are also more subtle evidences. The attraction of promotion at work might have as much to do with the prospect of a different chair or desk or room, than with all the doing aspects of the new post, or indeed the new relationships the job will open up. On a training course, some people will feel very short-changed if they do not leave the event with an armful of *things*. Relating people always seem to put someone else before their major decisions and considerations: 'What would he or she think' or 'How would it affect them?' So although they might well get involved in action and having or getting, they are more interested in what effect this will have on relationships. Then again, some people want *to be* settled or *to be* content or *to be* financially independent, and this seems to be predominant in the overall content of their lives.

Perhaps each of these feels familiar to you, and there is some part of each tendency in all of us, of course. But it is the *preference* that usually dictates how we behave, especially in important decisions and life changes. Knowing your preference means knowing yourself at a very basic level, and that is where excellence starts. So how can you establish your own 'life content' preference?

Discovering the contents of your life

If you cannot readily identify which of the five comes first in your life, and the order in which the others come, here is a simple exercise that should make it clear.

1 Start by asking yourself 'What is really important to me?' and write down your answer, expressing yourself *instinctively* rather than in carefully chosen words. Notice which content area your answer is in. Is it concerned with doing, knowing, getting/having, relating or being? You can usually tell by the words of your answer. If your desire is to sell more, it is clearly concerned with doing. If it is 'to have such and such', it is in the getting/having category. If it is to provide for your family, it is concerned with relating.

2 Then ask yourself, 'If I had that desire, fully and completely, then what?' Notice the answer that comes to mind and write it down. This again will probably be within one of the five content areas. For instance, you might say that by selling more I would *have* more money, or *get* that new car or house, therefore your *doing* is following by *getting*. The words we use tell us how we think.

3 Then, using your last answer, ask yourself again, 'If I had that desire, fully and completely, then what?' and again write down your answer. For instance, you might decide that by getting more money or the house of your choice, you would *be* happy or content. Here you have moved into the *being* category.

4 Ask the question once again, this time using your answer to step 3, and again write down the answer that comes to mind. If your answer to the last question was a content area you have not already written down, then repeat this step until you have a combination of content area cycles that brings you back to one you have already written down. That is, you have exhausted your own range of content areas and you have these in some order.

5 You now have a series of content areas for your life. For instance, doing to getting to being to relating.

6 Now return to step 1, and ask yourself again: 'What's really important to me?' As you think about this, ask yourself, 'Is there anything I need to do, know, get or have or relate or be, in order to get this?' and again notice the answer, if any, you give. If there is something further that comes to mind, it might well open up a different content area. For example, you might decide that in order to sell more you need to *know* more, which would involve some sort of training.

7 Now have a careful look at the combination of content areas you have written down. This is your personal pattern of life contents. It should feel immediately familiar, because you have probably followed this pattern time and time again in the past in major activities, work and family life. You may not have written down all five—and this is not important. What is important is that this is unique to you, including the order in which the contents appear.

You can now check the process once again, using different examples of what is important to you and going through the same exercise. You may be surprised that your cycle of life contents reappears in the same order, confirming that this indeed is the way you experience the content of your life. It is in effect your master strategy. Your preference will become apparent as your desires repeatedly fall into one category or another—you might confirm, for example, that you are a *doer* or a *getter*. But the syntax or sequence is just as important. A person might put doing or getting first to fulfil some *relating* or *being* goal which, to him or her, is more important. The same might apply in the above selling example, where in order to sell more a minimum of knowledge had to be acquired, even though the pleasure was in the doing or the getting.

By carrying out this exercise you will get to know yourself better. It explains some of the ways you have behaved in the past—behaviour that has resulted in what you are today and your successes.

Using your life contents self-knowledge

You can use this information in various forms. If you are to embark on some important activity in the future, you might be well advised to follow a pattern that has been successful in the past. For instance, if in the past you have been happier knowing about something before you have committed to doing it, it might be better not to short-cut this stage in the future. You might be able to recall times when you did miss one stage and came to grief—for example, because instinctively you need to know about things before you commit yourself either to doing or having.

You have therefore learned what is comfortable—what feels right—for you. But you might also reconsider whether you are happy with both the *weighting* and the order of your life contents. You might, for instance, want to place less importance on *getting* and *having*, and more on *knowing*. Or you might feel that you need to balance your life by *doing* much more, being more actively involved in things rather than being knowledgeable or just a 'passenger'. You may recognize the relating part of your life content as being rather weak, and consciously desire to weight it stronger. The *being* life content frequently comes at the end of the sequence, and this illustrates the hierarchy of goals that we met in Chapter 3, and which, for most individuals, culminates in outcomes like 'contentment', 'fulfilment' and 'personal happiness'—in other words, *being* what you want to be. You might determine that *being* will be the important aspect of your life. That being the case, and using what you have learned from NLP, you might well be able to bypass some of the other stages and reach the *being* state of mind that you desire. Note that the *being* category is predominantly a state of mind. One person, for example, feels financially secure in circumstances in which another would feel insecure; and one person is happy without the material possessions another person thinks are essential for happiness. The choice is yours, once you have gained knowledge of yourself by identifying your life contents.

Having considered your preference, and the weighting of your life contents, you might then wish to change the order of some of them to correct an imbalance you feel in your life. This might particularly apply, for instance, to a very active, doing person, and a person who is at the other extreme of having cerebral knowledge, but little experience. In the first case you might decide to put knowing first (including a bit of thinking and planning), and in the second case, get on and do things first.

Life contents in training

An understanding of this pattern can also help you to understand others, and gain the essential rapport that you need for effective communication. It will be immediately apparent, for instance, how these life content preferences affect learning and training. You will probably have met the trainees who want to get quickly involved in action—any action—rather than go through the drudgery of getting to know and understand things. You will also be familiar with trainees (and indeed trainers) who put *relating* very high on their list, and always seem concerned about what others think in the learning process. And others, again, who only seem concerned with the eventual certificate, or salary increase, or other *getting* or *having* that will result from a training event or programme.

Understanding life content cycles is thus vital in the design of any learning programme. At the very worst, we need to build in sufficient variety so that each trainee will benefit in some way. Just as it is possible to change sensory preferences by conscious practice, we can also change the life content cycle of others by skilful training programmes. The very awareness of one's personal cycle is a big start—as you will no doubt discover personally—and a trainee can be guided into giving more attention to other areas. Attention to this whole area of self-development gives weight to the *being* part of life content—which some argue is at the top of any hierarchy of goals— and should be an aspect of almost any training programme. That is, a trainee should not just finish up knowing more, or doing things better or even getting that cherished certificate, but should *be* a better manager, a better receptionist or a better person.

As I said earlier, it would be rare for any of these five aspects of life content to be missing from our past experience. Even the super-activist has some experience of knowing, and even the most passive introvert has memories of action that can be recalled. Therefore, any aspect of your life content cycle can be reinforced by reliving a memory when that characteristic was predominant, however isolated or far back in time the activity or event was experienced. By clear visualization of the experience—again going through the modalities and submodalities in the way we have already described—a particular aspect of your life is thus reinforced. We have already seen that, as far as your brain is concerned, you can 'create' experience by visualization. Thus you can add action, for instance, to a memory or future event short on action. Your behaviour then follows what you think—as sure as night follows day—so you *become* more active.

The mental rehearsal involved will also change your state of mind and attitude to a life content. By regular and clear visualization of *doing*, for instance, you might be more inclined to attempt new experiences when given the chance in the future, because your confidence has increased and your attitude has changed. Similarly, the state of mind conjured up by having to read a book, or acquire some essential knowledge before doing something, will come much easier after going through the mental process of recall and visualization.

These life content cycles tend to be long term macro strategies, and, like beliefs, have distant origins in our lives. But just as beliefs can be changed, we can also change these life content biases to meet our present-day outcomes. They can be made to fit what today we want to be and achieve. This is part of the personal choice that NLP seeks to open up. Mastery is all about understanding yourself and how you learn and behave. The life content cycle is a useful pattern that requires little imagination and creativity, so is accessible to the average 'left brain' professional, and is based on obvious common sense.

Strategy for creativity

Usually a person has a self-image which classifies him or her as being creative or non-creative, and like any self-belief this tends to be self-fulfilling. 'I'm not a terribly creative person' is the way this might emerge in conversation. As it has a powerful influence on our behaviour, a 'non-creative' person is under a handicap when he or she attempts to devise creative ideas in everyday situations and problem solving. With a little reflection, each of us will usually admit that there have been times in the past when we have been quite creative. Perhaps such occasions are not numerous, and they may have occurred outside the work context, but we can nevertheless recall them, and can indeed 'relive' them by making the modalities and submodalities of the experiences real. But we do not have to be creative all the time, and sometimes we need to have our feet firmly on the ground and be of a more critical frame of mind. In the same way, whether or not we consider ourselves to be either good critics or able to apply sound rational judgement, we can recall times in the past when we did indeed evaluate something critically, with some degree of excellence. By getting into the appropriate creative state of mind, we can become more creative at will in situations where this is demanded. Here is a simple exercise you can use to acquire your creative state of mind.

1 Identify some area you wish to solve or open up creatively and the outcome or goal you want to achieve, but do not think about it in detail. Then choose three physical places just in front of you that you can be ready to step into. One you will call the *dreamer* position, and one the *realist* position and one the *critic* position.

2 Now think of a time when you were really creative, when your dreamer, as we shall call it, generated some really creative choices. Then attempt to anchor this resourceful, creative state of mind and the strategies that you used, by stepping into your dreamer position and reliving that experience.

3 Recall a time when you thought very realistically and pragmatically and devised some plan to put an idea into action effectively. This is your super-organizer state. Anchor these resources and strategies to the realist position by stepping into it and reliving the experience.

4 Now identify a time when you criticized some plan or behaviour constructively. You were able to identify potential weaknesses and snags, but came up with possible alternatives that dealt with them effectively. Once again, anchor these resources—your inner critic— by stepping into the critic position and re-experiencing them.

5 Now, take the actual outcome that you are exploring, and step with it into your dreamer position. Access the state of mind that you experienced earlier and let your mind be free to accomplish your goal as a sequence of images. Conjure up as many alternative, creative ways of bringing about your outcome as you can. You can, of course, have recourse to the metaphors, chunking up and down, modelling, etc., we have already met.

6 Step into the realist position and become again the super-organizer, organizing your ideas into some implementable plan. Notice what you will need to do and change to make your earlier ideas realistic. Take each idea and seek to organize it in the best way possible.

7 Now step into the critic position and evaluate your plan. Ask questions about what has been overlooked and what is needed,

noticing the shortcomings in both the ideas themselves and also your plan for organizing and implementing them. Here you are likely to be listening to some inner voice, which is your familiar critic that keeps you right on such occasions.

8 Finally, go back to the dreamer position and, using all the information that was given to you by the realist and the critic, dream up new ideas that will overcome even the slightest objections. Carry on through the process once again, subjecting your most recent ideas to the realist and then to the critic, seeing if there are still any outstanding problems. If there are, step back once more into your dreamer position and start the entire process again.

Using this exercise, you are calling upon natural skills and states of mind that you have used successfully in the past. The reason why we often do not bring much creativity to a problem or situation is that our 'critic' and 'realist' are operating *at the same time* as the dreamer, so the dreamer tends to be suppressed. The critical part of the brain is the verbal, articulate part, so it tends to win in an argument, however weak its argument may be. The mute creative part rarely gets a fair hearing. If you have a low self-image as regards your creativity, this will also prevent you from being creative. By separating these different parts of ourselves, and allowing them to operate at their best separately, we can optimize the contribution of each, while maintaining congruence in the way we use them as a team.

The technique demands the skill of being able to remember situations in which you enjoyed particular states of mind, and being able to relive them as realistically as possible. As with other mental techniques, it helps to get into a relaxed frame of mind, and suspend left brain judgement. But all of these mental processes become easier with practice, so you can train yourself to do more or less what you want. Physical training also requires practice, but you are much less constrained when practising mentally than physically—so there effectively is no limit to what you can imagine.

Strategies

When modelling any behaviour, there are three essential elements, which are the 'success characteristics' we have already met.

1 The beliefs
2 The physiology of the behaviour
3 The strategies, or syntax.

At the level of an individual behaviour, or group of activities (such as giving a training presentation, spelling a word, or carrying out a task in a state of 'flow' or mastery) the strategy is the sequence of representations that drive the behaviour—the syntax, or order in which we carry it out. We also have strategies for *states* such as motivation, creativity and other attitudes or mental skills. These are described in the same thought language we used when accessing memories and in mental rehearsal. A motivation strategy, for example, might start with *seeing* the work that needs doing, and this is termed *visual external*, or V^e. You might then imagine what it will look like when it is finished—for instance, the tidy desk, or the reorganized filing system—and this is termed *visual internal constructed*, or V^{ic}. Third, you might recollect how satisfying it will feel to have completed the job, and this is termed *kinaesthetic internal remembered*, or K^{ir}. You might then tell yourself that it is time you started, and this is termed *auditory internal dialogue*, or A^{id}. Therefore, in this particular strategy, the sequence of representations is V^e, V^{ic}, K^{ir}, A^{id}. If you wanted to motivate a person with this particular strategy, you would follow his or her pattern. And if *you* wanted to be as motivated as that person, you would adopt the same strategy. For example, you would have a good look at what needed to be done, imagine visually how it would appear when it was finished, enjoy the feeling of the job well done, then tell yourself—an internal dialogue—to get started. This, of course, is just one unique strategy, so your first action is to find the person on whom to model yourself.

We usually find excellence only in different fields—one person might be an excellent model of organization, another of creativity, another person might be a high-speed reader or clever with numbers. So you do not have to find an all-round genius as a model for your desired strategy, but rather someone who excels in your chosen activity. As we have seen, you can also use your own memory resource to elicit your own strategy, thinking back to a time when you were highly motivated and imagine the sequence of sights, sounds and feelings, both internal and external.

Eliciting strategies

To elicit a strategy, you first identify some specific behaviour, and get the person to either carry out the behaviour or re-experience in his or her imagination a time when that behaviour was being enacted. This re-experiencing should be in an associated form—the person should imagine that he or she is actually doing the behaviour, rather than watching from the outside. Try to identify the very first thing the person is aware of as he or she enters into the cycle of behaviour that you want to elicit, and find out the representation system that was being used. Is it external or internal? Is the person triggered by something in the outside world that can be seen, heard or felt, or does the trigger seem to come from inside (such as an inner voice, memory or feeling). And if internal, is it something remembered or constructed? Ask what the person was next aware of, and again identify this in the form of a representation—that is, a visual, auditory or kinaesthetic experience. Usually habitual behaviour is carried out in an unconscious or semi-conscious state, so we are not aware of these complex strategies, even though we use them continuously. Therefore, questioning may be needed. Keep a check on any clues as to which modalities your model is using. Listen, for instance, to the predicates—

the words and phrases used—and watch for the eye accessing cues that we have already met. Usually you have to keep reverting to an earlier part of the strategy sequence to ensure that he or she has not missed a stage. Keep asking the question 'Was there anything you were aware of before that?' until the description of the person's strategy seems to be complete and fits his or her experience.

You have already met the idea of submodalities, and these play an important part in this elicitation process. For example, a big, bright, close-up visualization of an outcome will usually have a very different impact on our behaviour than a small, dark, distant one. The way to install or adopt a strategy is to do it. Experiment, and apply the strategy you have elicited from your model. Future pace it—run it through your imagination as if you were actually experiencing it, then start to apply your empowering states and skills in real life. The only real test then is, does it work? If it doesn't, you are free to elicit and try further strategies until you get the outcome you want.

Sorting categories and criteria

There are other macro strategies, like life contents, that are usually seen as an aspect of a person's personality, affecting all their outlook and behaviour. In some cases there are verbal patterns that allow us to recognize these strategies, and this can be particularly helpful in gaining rapport and in better communication. These patterns reflect the categories by which we personally sort, and the criteria or values that we use. When establishing a new relationship you may have little or no knowledge of the person's interests, such as a hobby or pastime, so there are limits in the connections you can make to bring about rapport. However, we each use common sorting categories such as:

- place
- time
- people
- activity
- information
- things
- age
- numbers.

These categories are much more universal than special interests (such as stamp collecting or cats), and once we can spot the categories a person uses, we can begin to use the appropriate sorting language. The words a person uses will be a clue to his or her strategy for categorizing, just as we were able to determine sensory preference by predicates. One person might describe a holiday, for example, by a whole series of *places*—descriptions of villages, towns, buildings. Another person will describe the same sort of holiday, but in terms of *people* they have met, or related with. Another person will simply give a list of *things* they have done, the activities and so on. Thus, whatever the person's interests, items are arranged in a particular, consistent way. Once we identify this pattern, we can, with a little bit of flexibility, make a connection with the person's sorting preference and thus establish and build on rapport.

Every time we open our mouths we communicate the sort of categories that we use, and criteria that we apply. You can find out how others think by asking simple questions, or even just by listening. Knowing what matters to people, you understand more about their map of reality, and so can build up rapport. Once you can identify your own strategy, you have the choice to change, just as in the other life contents model. By identifying another person's strategy, you have the knowledge to become a master communicator, establishing immediate rapport by literally speaking that person's language.

By building up skills in recognizing sorting categories and criteria—thinking strategies—we can build up very powerful communication skills. The secret of good communication is rapport, and this is yet another way of establishing a vital connection. We can also model successful strategies.

Appendix

Further reading

Harry Alder, *The Right Brain Manager*, Piatkus, 1993.

Harry Alder, *NLP: The New Art and Science of Getting What You Want*, Piatkus, 1994.

Harry Alder, *Think Like a Leader*, Piatkus, 1995.

Steve Andreas and Charles Faulkner (editors), *NLP: The Technology of Achievement*, NLP Comprehensive, 1994.

Richard Bandler and John Grinder, *Frogs into Princes*, Real People Press, 1979.

Richard Bandler and John Grinder, *Reframing*, Real People Press, 1982.

Richard Bandler, *Using Your Brain for a Change*, Real People Press, 1985.

Joseph O'Connor and John Seymour, *Introducing Neuro-Linguistic Programming*, Harper Collins, 1990.

Maxwell Maltz, *Psychocybernetics*, Simon and Schuster, 1960.

Anthony Robbins, *Unlimited Power*, Simon and Schuster, 1986.

Short glossary

Associated   Seeing an experience as if through your own eyes.

Chunking   Going down or up a level, respectively, to see a situation in more detail or from a wider perspective.

Complex equivalence   Two statements that are meant to mean the same thing (e.g. 'she walked past me, she is annoyed').

Content reframing   Focusing on another part or aspect of a statement or experience to give it a different meaning (What else could this mean?).

Context reframing   Changing the context of a statement or experience to give it a different meaning (In what other context would this be appropriate?).

Dissociated   Seeing an experience as if through someone else's eyes—from outside yourself.

Downtime   The state when your attention is on your own inner thoughts, e.g. when preoccupied or daydreaming.

Ecology   Used in NLP as the relationship between the various thoughts and behaviours of an individual, including that person's different outcomes.

First position   Perceiving the world from your own point of view, rather than as someone else sees things (*see also* 'Second position' and 'Third position').

Future pacing   Mentally rehearsing a future outcome to help bring it about.

Meta Model   A model that identifies imprecise language patterns and gives questions and responses to clarify or challenge them.

Mirroring   Matching other people's behaviour to bring about rapport.

Mismatching   Adopting different behaviour patterns, thus breaking rapport (e.g. to end a conversation).

Modal Operator of Necessity   A Meta Model term that includes rules involving, 'should', 'ought', etc.

Neurological levels   Different levels of experience: environment, behaviour, capability, belief, identity.

Perceptual positions   Different viewpoints as in first, second and third perceptual positions.

Predicates   Words expressing the use of a representational system; e.g. 'it sounds OK'.

Presuppositions   Statements that have to be taken for granted if a communication is to make sense.

Reframing   Changing the frame of reference round a statement or experience to give it another meaning.

Representation system   How we code sensory information internally, using vision, hearing, feelings, taste and smell.

Second position   Seeing things from another person's point of view (*see also* 'First position' and 'Third position').

Strategy   A sequence of thought and behaviour that brings about a certain outcome.

Submodality   The qualities and characteristics of our representation systems, e.g. the size and brightness of an internal image.

Third position   The perspective of a detached outside observer (*see also* 'First position' and 'Second position').

Timeline   The way we represent time, storing pictures of our past, present and future.

Universal quantifiers   A Meta Model language term that includes words such as 'every', 'all' and 'never'.

Uptime   A state of focused attention, where the senses are used outwardly rather than inwardly.

Index

Further titles in the McGraw-Hill Training Series

WORKSHOPS THAT WORK
100 Ideas to Make Your Training Events More Effective
Tom Bourner, Vivien Martin, Phil Race
ISBN 0-07-707800-4

THE HANDBOOK FOR ORGANIZATIONAL CHANGE
Strategy and Skill for Trainers and Developers
Carol A. O'Connor
ISBN 0-07-707693-1

TRAINING FOR PROFIT
A Guide to the Integration of Training in an Organization's
Success
Philip Darling
ISBN 0-07-707786-5

TEAM BUILDING
A Practical Guide for Trainers
Neil Clark
ISBN 0-07-707846-2

DEVELOPING MANAGERS AS COACHES
A Trainer's Guide
Frank Salisbury
ISBN 0-07-707892-6

THE ASSERTIVE TRAINER
A Practical Guide for Trainers
Liz Willis and Jenny Daisley
ISBN 0-07-707077-2

MEETING MANAGEMENT
A Manual of Effective Training Material
Leslie Rae
ISBN 0-07-707782-2

LEARNING THROUGH SIMULATIONS
A Guide to the Design and Use of Simulations in Business and
Education
John Fripp
ISBN 0-07-707588-9 paperback
ISBN 0-07-707789-X Disk

IMAGINATIVE EVENTS Volumes I & II
A Sourcebook of Innovative Simulations, Exercises, Puzzles
and Games
Ken Jones
ISBN 0-07-707679-6 Volume I
ISBN 0-07-707680-X Volume II
ISBN 0-07-707681-8 Set Ringbinder

TRAINING TO MEET THE TECHNOLOGY CHALLENGE
Trevor Bentley
ISBN 0-07-707589-7

CLIENT-CENTRED CONSULTING
A Practical Guide for Internal Advisers and Trainers
Peter Cockman, Bill Evans and Peter Reynolds
ISBN 0-07-707685-0

TOTAL QUALITY TRAINING
The Quality Culture and Quality Trainer
Brian Thomas
ISBN 0-07-707472-6

CAREER DEVELOPMENT AND PLANNING
A Guide for Managers, Trainers and Personnel Staff
Malcolm Peel
ISBN 0-07-707554-4

DESIGNING AND ACHIEVING COMPETENCY
A Competency-based Approach to Developing People and
Organizations
Edited by Rosemary Boam and Paul Sparrow
ISBN 0-07-707572-2

SELF-DEVELOPMENT
A Facilitator's Guide
Mike Pedler and David Megginson
ISBN 0-07-707460-2

DEVELOPING WOMEN THROUGH TRAINING
A Practical Handbook
Liz Willis and Jenny Daisley
ISBN 0-07-707566-8

HOW TO SUCCEED IN EMPLOYEE DEVELOPMENT
Moving from Vision to Results
Ed Moorby
ISBN 0-07-707459-9

MAKING MANAGEMENT DEVELOPMENT WORK
Achieving Success in the Nineties
Charles Margerison
ISBN 0-07-707382-7

MANAGING PERSONAL LEARNING AND CHANGE
A Trainer's Guide
Neil Clark
ISBN 0-07-707344-4

THE BUSINESS OF TRAINING
Achieving Success in Changing World Markets
Trevor Bentley
ISBN 0-07-707328-2

All books are published by:

McGraw-Hill Book Company Europe
Shoppenhangers Road, Maidenhead, Berkshire SL6 2QL, England
Tel: (01628) 23432   Fax: (01628) 770224